NOT NOT A JEW

A Novella In Verst

ALISON LESLIE GOLD

TMI Publishing, Providence, RI

www.tmipublishing.com

Author's website: www.AlisonLeslieGold.com
https://facebook.com/Alison Leslie Gold

Not Not a Jew

TMI Publishing
61 Doyle Avenue
Providence, RI 02906
www.tmipublishing.com

Cover by Hanaan Rosenthal

ISBN: 978-1-938371-24-0
Previous Edition ISBN: 978-1-938371-22-6

Author Blog

www.AlisonLeslieGold.com

Also by Alison Leslie Gold

Nonfiction

*Anne Frank Remembered: The Story of the Woman who Helped
to Hide the Frank Family (with Miep Gies)*
Memories of Anne Frank: Reflections of a Childhood Friend
Fiet's Vase and Other Stories of Survival, Europe 1939-1945
A Special Fate: Chiune Sugihara: Hero of the Holocaust
Lost and Found
Love in the Second Act

Fiction

The Potato Eater
Clairvoyant
The Devil's Mistress
The Woman Who Brought Matisse Back from the Dead
Elephant in the Living Room (with Darin Elliott)

*Look for **Alison Leslie Gold** on Facebook*
*Author Blog: **www.AlisonLeslieGold.com***

TABLE OF CONTENTS

VERST BY VERST

Why leave Berlin for Paris? An unemployed man with no friends, Eli G., with a wife, Vera, and one child to feed, Karl, got fifty-one mark a month (1931) in relief. Vera budgeted:

Per month = 51 mark

rent, electricity, heat, outings = 32.50 mark
feed family = 18.50 mark

Per day

½ loaf bread
2 ½ kilo potatoes
100 grams cabbage
50 grams margarine

Per adult per day

2 potatoes
5 slices bread
knob margarine
fistful cabbage
herring on 2 Sundays out of 4

Child per day

½ liter milk

herring on 3 Sundays out of 4

Young and foreign, Eli had been a member of the Red Front Fighters' League in the Wedding District when he caught sight of Vera, a bright-eyed medical student who wanted to find a cure for all cancers. He was at a meeting on Bülowplatz at Karl Liebknecht House. After the meeting, Eli, Eleazer, Baruch and Shmerl and other members of the Red Front kicked a makeshift soccer ball around the square. Eli missed a kick when he turned to gape at orange curling hair. From far off Vera was a friendly, hovering humming-bird.

Eli asked Shmerl, Who is she?

Shmerl answered without hesitation, Her dialectic is razor sharp.

Flying backwards with him away from Viktoria Park, Vera didn't resist.

In Eli's basement room under an emerald-colored ceiling, Vera cast a long shadow. Their male child clamored, lifted his fists. That day thirty-one people were murdered by the police in the square, Eli had seen it, seen a policeman crush a worker's skull with a truncheon. With bare hands, his *Arbeiter Illustrierte Zeitung* tucked under his arm, more afraid than ever before in his life, he scooped brain matter from the bashed skull when the police began to chase him. He ran into the underground station, got on the first car, changed trains at Friedrichsfelde-Alexanderplatz Station. He used the coin meant for margarine to buy a single ticket into the Titania Palace Cinema, the grand theater with parabolic surfaces. The Titania Palace: Light-enhanced bronzes. Light-enhanced silver dome. Light-enhanced lacquered walls. Light-enhanced claret velvet upholstery. The film flickered. Eli sat in the dark and set the weighty cap on his lap. The film – *Helgas Fall und Aufstieg.* He drank in Greta Garbo's large and moving lips. His own face was on fire. He wondered, Why is it ending like this? Have the police followed me? Will they crush my skull next? Experiencing heart palpitations in flocks, he mumbled, *Ha-Tikvah,* and withdrew his only cigar from his pocket but couldn't strike the wooden match because his hands were sticky. Another wave of palpitations rippled left to right.

His mother's ghost took the unlit cigar and dropped it between his legs. He smelled his hand, smelled kerosene, scorched chicken's feet, medicine against lice. The smell was the smell of the *chedar* (study house) in summer, the strong human odor floating over the study table where he had once sat daily squeezed beside the son of Baal Shem, who cut oak trees. When the *melamed* (teacher) whacked the woodcutter's son's hand with a green stick, the boy's *kartuz* (cap) once fell against the Torah and sawdust spilled onto the Torah. The *melamed* hit Eli on the side of the head too. He instructed Eli to recite psalms in sing-song. Memories of leftover *miltz* (spleen) stuffed with flour and raw onions leaked from time past. In that dark theater, a painting visited him, a self-portrait as a map of the skull inside out, a spleen-like brain. He lifted the cap, felt the weight of human brains, a worker's brain. He was overcome with ideology. Fierce ideology was an atmosphere, a slow chord in a storm—spellbinding, suspenseful—a splash of crimson against monochrome. I'll never waver, he thought, his pulse twitching. Garbo's eyelids closed, Eli closed his too, shuffled colors and images as he would a deck of cards. Gray. Topaz. Snow. Neuro-blossoms. White radishes. Electric charges like hummingbirds shot straight up, hovered, beat rapid wings. His brain plumped like a squid shooting a cloud of sepia and spread into gray crevices. Growing soggier and heavier, the juices were beginning to leak. I've snubbed Cubist ideas, blusterers, I've avoided feeding frenzies, he thought with glacial pride. He conjured mangoes and orchids, numbers and balance sheets, white trousers, a stiff silk shirt.

He turned the brain matter upside down onto the floor between his shoes and squeezed out the juice from his hat. Having unraveled his ball of twine from that settlement in the east all the way to Berlin on foot, Eli conjured Vera's vulva in Paris. Karl, our boy, will speak French to us. His molar was loose and moved with the tap of his tongue. In my settlement, I could still be a water carrier, wood hewer, coachman, beggar, tailor, shoemaker or rabbi. I could gossip at the well, be whiskered. I could walk among geese, ducks, calves, goats, chickens and cats. Never dogs. I could walk into Mama's kitchen and push my head against her rock-hard bosom. In a dream he had visited his mother, bitten her bottom with his teeth while smelling a faint odor from her anus. He sat in the dark in Berlin, hatching a plan: Leave Berlin by Yom Kippur. Forsake herring. Climb out of the hourglass with Vera and Karl. Cross vast swatches of primary color by train. Draw a thick black line west, make a pathway toward Fauves, Cubists, half-Cubists, Picasso, Cézanne, Braque worship. Make a flat, shapeless black line, a grid, a containment. He was overheated and thirsty while needle-sharp pains from parasites made dogged stabs, wrenching and spilling, sputtering, rooted inside. Because of his upbringing, he knew the correct way to put on his shoes in the morning. Papa had called him chosen but said he was worse than a dog. All through his remembered *bar mitzvah* ceremony he'd thought about food because he'd eaten nothing except raisins and walnuts. He thought about how he would kiss a grown woman's lips. When his name was called, he chanted the benediction first, then, read a Bible lesson, then, a verse from the Torah scroll. His speech was short indeed: There is grave signification in this occasion for me. The rabbi blessed him. Eli searched the congregation for Papa's beard among beards. Papa's face was hallowed now. Eli stared down the *melamed*. He detested the man who had hit him with a stick every day for six years. He swore: Never again will I enter this place. If I see the *melamed* on the road I'll belt him. He evoked: Moses! Hear!

Vera warned him, One should not sneer! Your glands could fail! We might not make good use of our glands. I have a strong wish to stay in Berlin. I've endured my lecturer's goatee. I've engaged Herr Professor in conversation. I even dared to tell him, Imagine zinc being dropped into sulfuric acid and nothing happening? If Einstein is right, the angles of a triangle do not add up to two right angles. And, when I told him this, Herr Professor nodded, *Nu*.

Again she entreated him, Please let's stay in Berlin!

Eli ate while Karl slept in the crook of his arm.

Euclid may be wrong by a few millionths of an inch. Don't laugh, it's not a detective story.

Was it? The triangle—the crime, the angels—witnesses.

Stop reading Marx. Read Zola, Tolstoy, Vera badgered.

Eli poured schnapps into the teapot, swatted at flies with his dog-eared *Das Kapital*.

You're the accomplice to capitalists, he badgered back.

Slyly he teased her away from her textbook. The temperature was dropping, heaps of snow and ice were piled under their single window and there was nothing in the sugar bowl with which to settle the coal bill. On the wall above the bed, Eli's map of the world, four months' work: Berlin, Paris, Constantinople, Alaska, Mexique, Perou, minute Indies, Chine, Large Russie, Groenland. Archepel Bismark in black gouache. Within orange borders were patterns—olives, grapes, human heads, ivy leaves.

Nothing was left for a drink at The White Mouse Cabaret after Eli splurged on carp outside the covered market on Dircksenstrasse off Alexanderplatz. He bought carp wrapped in newspaper, not briquettes from the coal cart, not beer, because of the brewery strike. Their clothing had frozen on the clothesline. Vera pinned the carp there too. Comestibility of blue overalls, of half-eaten carp, a cat's cradle of ice thread had spun between the overalls and the carp. Vera pulled back her hair and tied it with a black bow. Often she got goose pimples along her arms. She had distracted ultramarine eyes that were getting short-sighted.

Ten canvases rested against the wall, three years' work. Again he decided to leave Berlin.

Why must we leave here? she shouted. I'm against it.

Eli coated her nipples with flour and water paste, slapped on newspaper strips and smoothed around and round the curves. Eli's elegant, wizard's hands were doughy. Vera longed for sour cream. A swatch of spangled rug lay across her lap sewn with green thread, the design of Neptune's trident.

Why uproot?

She tried another tactic, turned her angular pleading face toward his, Why?

His reply, lifted from Marx, "*To transform the world…*",
wean us away from cottage cheese and herring.

Red herring?

No, herring in cream.

I would gladly sacrifice to taste sharp onions and
bay leaf with coriander corn. Please stay put, she
begged.

On charity, both leaner than greyhounds, Eli
spoke Berlin German while Vera spoke function-
al high German. Her mother had spoken it too.
Vera was professorial, not inquisitive. Eli's pale face,
even paler since the police had chased him into the
U-Bahn – *Indi gasn, tsu di masn* (into the streets, to
the masses). He painted using scarlet, gold, crimson,
cadmium yellow colors, designed perimeters with
small diamonds, rectangles, ovals, trellis shapes, the
topography of Perou. Karl howled out for milk but
could not drink because Vera's *papier-maché* covered
breasts had not dried. On Karl's little red vest was
Eli's design from Cézanne's boy. Eli had given Karl
a fat brush handle to suck on that made him giddy
from linseed oil. His saucy eyes targeted Vera while
he stood like a plump heron on her lap, chirping
for more, naturally imperious. His every move was
watched by four eyes, two behind owl eyeglasses.
Karl scowled when more was not forthcoming and
pulled her hair of oranges.

✦

Tangled in the new French language, aloof Vera burrowed into the trunk. The iron gray of winter filtered not enough light to see the sperm swatch left on the hem of her dress. She reached for the spice box molded like a poppy on a shapely stem. Its base, a flat triangle made of silver with a bird on it. She touched her biscuit mold, tin-plated, fish-shaped, then the gingerbread mold, rectangular with carved ornamentation of jug, rhombus, leaves that had the Hebrew letter *shin* on the edge. These objects were friends to her fingertips. Reaching deeper she lifted her prize – the wooden saltcellar belonging to Mama's Mama's Mama. It was a square box with a high back crammed with decorations: In front, a Star of David, on the left side, a single rosette, on the right side, a lion and a unicorn, on its back, houses, hunters, an eagle, a wolf, a dog. On the side rim were human and animal shapes in relief. On the reverse side, a human figure wearing a crown and under the figure the inscription: *Eat a morsel with salt. A house. A hunter. An eagle. A wolf. A dog.* This was (in a manner of speaking) her dowry. Also in the trunk, letters from Mama and Papa tied together with string written for them by the rabbi.

Prickly, Vera wiped her relics and lumped them on the kitchen shelf. Hair in plaits, she boiled potatoes on the gas cooker, their laundry cooking in the same big pot. The two rooms in Paris were slovenly. Surely it was a blunder to have come away from Berlin. She sliced onions, was starting over, not one cloud in the sky, was hopeful that they would sometime be carried aloft in chairs by twelve strong friends.

In a combative mood, Vera challenged Eli, For what? We're living on potatoes, love-making in the 12th Arrondissement.

They lived on rue Rouvet, heard trains clanging night and day, stayed free of politics. Three paintings are invited to a show at rue Denfert–Rachereau Gallery, Eli bragged. I've much to prepare in the New Year.

With six other refugee painters! she hissed over the train noise. So what's the big deal?

The factory whistle tooted. It was a morbid morning, she was sharp-tongued again, scanning the empty larder for what wasn't there, myopic in the gloom because her glasses were no longer right. She didn't know that cobwebs had caught in her hair or that their papers were forged. The canvas with thick impastoed paint attracted grime and flecks. She was homesick, galled when misunderstood in monosyllabic French, called herself a cuckoo. Perspiring because of the stoked stove in the tiny airless studio, Eli's model was himself. He looked at his own face in the mirror, saw an enlarged head, averted eyes, dilated hammer-and-sickle pupils. He bent to sip vodka mixed with honey then squeezed the glass onto the narrow table top cluttered with materials, colors, tubes. Above it were shelves piled with painting/maps of Cracovie, Varsovie, Smolensk, Vitebsk,

Minsk, Odessa, Gomel, Orgeyev (Bessarabia) Smilovitchi. He painted nothing but maps often against mustard egg-yellow backgrounds. Fed up, he sank onto their bed, raised his knees up, the legs encased in blue mechanic's overalls that were bald at the knees. He wore red and white patterned socks. Also spats.

Pieces of white marble, bronze, limestone, and hand-polished slate were lumped against the wall under the stone arch connected to the barrel-vaulted roof by a damp, mildewed pillar. Eli dipped two-day-old brioche into yesterday's *vin de pays*, his face a leering gargoyle when he bit the rock-hard roll causing the molar to crumble. He dropped the brioche into the glass to let it soften. He could feel bits of broken enamel with his tongue as he held a *papier-maché* bust and wiped his wide forehead with it. The bust had a gigantic coiled anaconda snake base that was misshapen by a swollen lump. The Anaconda's heavy lunch (an entire pig swallowed whole) whose shape was outlined at the center of the bulge. Outside, the taxi meter was ticking, ticking.

The concierge called Eli *Paille-au-Nex* (strawnose). Eli's broken speech reeked of onion. Needing asylum was written all over him. He had been unable to paint, had gone out walking. He cadged an oyster from a big basket close to the Hôtel de la Haute Loire, paused to listen to *Crazy Rhythms, Crazy Blues* leaking into the street. Oyster deep in his pocket, he hurried toward home to relieve Vera of Karl, his grain of sand. Vera was due at the laboratory where her asymmetrical crystals rotated left and right in polarized light. She called these micro-organisms vital even when putrefied. When Vera rambled on about the laboratory, her cheeks flushed crimson, whetting Eli's eyes. He hurried down the stony street, jelly-hearted. Bred bulldogs skidded across the icy stone. One heavy breather was annihilated by a passing taxi before Eli's eyes. I've not been taken under the arm of Paris, he admitted to himself, gazing up at the buildings of smelly cheese, the clusters of purple grapes.

Eli's coat was tattered as much as the beggar standing beside the cathedral door. He was tallow-faced like the cherubs and cupids he drew. He turned the corner, the street narrowed, he turned again, entered a thoroughfare from which geometric spoked streets radiating. In a shop window were crusty baguettes, a giant clam, an eel in oil, also a chameleon perched on the rim of a white coffee cup whose tongue shot out and in. His stomach squeezed with hunger. Crossing the intersection, he saw hundreds of blond heads popping from holes in the stone. No *déjeuner*, no *digestifs*, no *cassis*, no *pastis*. He hoped Vera had prepared onion soup, to be followed by lovemaking, then *siesta* with locked legs, fingers entwined. Only after that would he let her go to work.

The unopened letter leaned up against the wash-tub. Inside, two kopeks, date of death, cause of death, an egg laid on a holiday. Vera's Papa was dead. Eli painted *crème-de-menthe* on the trees, on moths, on butterflies, on fifteen small paintings scattered on scraps. Slyly he squeezed a fat tube. He inhaled the smells of turpentine, lavender, resin, harangued captive Karl, "*Man will be stronger, wiser, subtler, his body will become harmonized.*"

He repeated "harmonized" and flicked off a dangling worm of paint.

The average human, you, me, will rise to the heights of Aristotle, Goethe, Marx, Trotsky. "*Above the high ridge new peaks will rise.*" So says Leon Trotsky. So says Leon Trotsky.

Karl kicked turpentine from the tin onto the letter, sloshed on the spill with bare feet.

Your mother is a reactionary, Eli informed their son.

Karl pranced across his father's drawings, left wet footprints, so Eli picked up the wet drawings and pinned them on the wall to dry out. He explained, "*From each according to his abilities, to each according to his needs.*" So says Karl Marx.

He kissed Karl's streaked face and saw that his Lucifer red feet had broken out in a rash. From a potbellied brown bottle of Benedictine, Eli poured yellow brimstone into a glass, letting a drop spill onto the mélange that Karl strolled upon again with pleasure. They nibbled resin-soaked brioche along with garlic-laced ratatouille. Dancing tango-like through

the room, magnet fields of morosity hovered above
father and son. Below, in the first strata of earth, were
fossils, ferns, fuel. Karl let out a silver-toned belch
and wrapped his arms around Eli's knees. He bit Eli's
hand when Eli tried to lift him onto the bed made of
two chairs next to the stove. Karl's fingernails turned
white, his sand-colored hair and apricot ears stood
out. Eyes grew out of onions in a bag kept under the
bed-chair. Pressing Karl's head against the thread-
bare satin pillow, Eli swiped at smudges around his
mouth, ran his thumb down Karl's backbone, was
awed by his warm aura. Absorbing his offspring, in
optical concentration, the mongrel outline of Karl's
head memorialized him. Eli held Karl's testicles aloft
in the flat of his paint-smudged hand. He sat beside
the washtub full of pungent laundry in washing soda
delighted that the testicles were periwinkle blue,
glossy, like polished marble lettuces.

✦

Limpet, clinging, Vera called him, Pig. Pig with
small hands. The candle dripped into day-old bread.
She hadn't meant it. The lit gas lamp hissed while
she served frugal noodle soup, sunflower seeds and
cucumbers. In Karl's hand, Vera's fountain pen
(filled with brown ink) forging passes. Eli smacked
the side of Karl's head with an open palm while Vera
watched every stroke of the pen, wary of mistakes,
of noodle drips. Karl was lanky but with a large

neck, had thick fingers, was a natural counterfeiter. He wore white trousers with a striped sailor shirt, abhorred supervision but held his tongue. The brown ink, from the twenty-three karat gold nib on Vera's pen (pearl with black veins) flowed like a tonic.

Karl mumbled, We're godforsaken.

Vera avoided being discursive while Eli cleaned brushes by wiping them on newsprint. His eyes tangling sumptuously with her eyes above Karl's head, saw a crumb of Eros stuck in the corner of Vera's eye. Comportment was included in the price of admission, so she gave a sinuous thrust of her hips. Karl stopped the clock, capped the pen. A lump of impatience was stuck in his throat. All the while pounding rain washed against the shuttered and bolted window. Karl had no strong defense against their bickering nor their wet lusts. He had a two-parent theory: Impact between Eli, comet, Vera, earth, and himself, collision fragment. He believed he was held to them by gravitational force and revolved like a spinning acrobat around them in filial momentum, the leaf (his heart) turning toward and away from the sun.

Boil water. Boil water. No letters came anymore. From anywhere. The last news: The cousin thrown from a moving train, a last pleading request for help/ money/ticket to Malkinia or Bialystok. *...sell the pen, sell the spice box shaped like a poppy on a stem, it's made of silver and has a bird on top.* Their gas masks were under the porcelain stove. Paris had become a fortress.

Karl reassured Vera *sotto voce*, If Le Havre is burning, take apples, take eggs.

In the lab, Vera worked with white blood cells. She rubbed her smudged owl glasses with the hem of her skirt while charting antibodies, injecting fertilized eggs of mice, keeping data until a termination letter arrived.

Class enemy! Eli hissed about the owner of the laboratory.

Eli sketched Vera's face with a burnt matchstick on a discarded box of Gitanes, firing the match for a second and third time, to make a new charcoal stub each time. He sketched Karl's face on top of the first, shortened Karl's nose. How to appease three growling stomachs? How not to leave Paris? Reaching into Vera's ocher handbag, he felt for coins. The cracked molar cried out for schnapps. In the street below, the willows and poplars along rue Rouver cast shade across cobbles wet from another punishing rainstorm (1940). He counted coins enough for potatoes, candles, a silk ribbon for Vera's hair.

He and Vera smelled sewer stench at the intersection of the Jazz Bar. My kingdom for a mouthful of stinging schnapps, a clove to hold against my aching tooth. A refrain faded in and out: *Why do you whisper? Why tell the trees? Whispering trees. Why tell them all your secrets? Why tell who you kissed long ago? Blabbering trees...* American music, warbling voices, people dancing but not in rhythm. Eli stroked Vera's back. Kisling was in Marseille, Bondy's diabetes was (said to be) running rampant. Most seditious urges had subsided as had origins. Nationality was blurred at the edge but, had it been blurred enough?

Connu comme?

Not Cravovie. Not Karsovie. Not Smolensk. Not Vitebsk or Minsk. Like Kisling's *Map* in various colors, Allemagne blurred and dissolving.

The ferrets were gray-green with puffed caps. Unshaven Eli had left his wife and child asleep. Three cars were shunted onto the engine. Pajamas were folded around a bottle of wine in his shabby bag. In it also were crusts of bread, one hard-boiled egg, an apple with wrinkled skin. He was fearful of derailment. Gnats swarmed in the sun's vomit that splashed against the window glass. He heard grisly chimes playing up and down the corridor. The porter wore gabardine, the steward a short white jacket, both were hurrying along the corridor just as Eli had toward Komsomol meetings – the locomotive of history, of revolution. The compartment filled. One each: Cro-Magnon (French) Man, Neanderthal (German) Man, Heidelberg (German) Man, all cupping undefended groins when the whistle sounded on entering the tunnel. Having arranged themselves in a parabola, these men sat like statues with fat and hair. The pressured rush hurt Eli's ears. The train was at least three hours from any custom office. One of the men continually pulled the end of his mus-

tache. Every movement aggrieved Eli. Though only
a verst or two from Paris, he felt in ruin, unshaven,
no wolf. When pounding artillery could be heard,
he didn't loosen the knotted pea-green cravat but,
forsaking the apple and wine, Eli exited the compartment and dropped off the back of the train into a
field. *Voilà.*

A cold wind puffed up his cassock. He was sor-
ry for no one, inconvenienced, rattled, wiped his
eyes with the hem of the garment. Red, yellow and
brown leaves covered the field of wooden crosses that
was ablaze with autumn. Beyond: the encampment.
Having cramp after cramp, he needed to relieve
himself and soon. Crouching down while waiting for
the platoon to blow up the bridge, tears poured from
his eyes. When perturbation calmed enough he knotted the rope, renewed like an adolescent. The color
red leaked from the vermilion-and-black marbled
sky while vegetable shapes dominated the horizon.
These were deceiving shapes, rocking clown-like,
jerking back and forth as if on rockers. The swallows
came back smelling of cheese, *haleh* in their beaks.
Stepping on shells and seaweed, Eli held onto the
boathook. Finally, he was able to relieve himself in
deep water that swarmed with frogs, snails, geolo-
gy. In his pocket was an invitation for bouillabaisse
that hadn't been prepared by the retreating army of
de Gaulle but by the Minister of Culture for Vichy
artists. Misery passed. He needed to relieve himself

again. Still a garlanded silhouette, he climbed into the birdcage, hyphenated his conscience.

Hands sticky, tongue coated, Eli tip-toed through the woody embankment. No patrols had passed but he was so fear-filled, his perorations broke into fragments. A wide-brimmed hat obscured sallow cheeks and a twitching nerve. Hearing more artillery, he raised both arms high, was so shaky he broke off a branch to use as a crook. Ossified by fear, he thought that his penis might turn green or orange or violet. At the road a car with blue paint on its headlights, mattress roped to its roof, passed by. Was it true that the Germans had doused the population with a powder that made people stupid? The village came into view. It was nearly deserted except for a few lowing cows. As directed, he found a path to the black market where he traded the ration of nine twenty-fifths of a kilo of sausage to the imperialist marketer for coal and gouache, tried not to look at the face. Back at zero, he hurried away, floating like a mushroom gatherer. He munched a small lump of unripened cheese. Cypresses and pines spread their branches above him. He was homesick for kitchen dialect but hurried like a weasel toward the Pantheon instead of the smuggler's route into Spain. The weighty horizon pressed against his back, there was a potato field ahead. He had a pocket full of tomorrow's currency: uneasiness, woe, necessity, sandbags.

Another molar split. Pain brought a policeman in a tin helmet astride Eli's back as well as a milkman who dropped clanging cans onto cobblestones. A gas mask in its khaki case cuffed his ear. Two soldiers leaned against the front of the Taverne Alsacienne picking gristle from between their teeth. They'd never seen an avocado, never owned boots before, never tasted asparagus. Watching the man in harrowing pain clutching his fists to his jawbone, the lineaments stretched. Eli's last coin fell into a cleft in the cobbled stone. A bystander watched the moisture flow down Eli's neck. By sheer will it condensed, then evaporated. Eli crossed his arms over his chest, uncrossed them, stood back. Snowflakes sprang soundlessly from the heavens. The soldiers walked on. The policeman gripped Eli's shoulder.

Mon Dieu!

The milkman dropped two sous into his hands that smelled of verbena.

V'n wie kimmt Ihr? (Where do you come from?)

A bitter yet curative pill. To think he was hearing Yiddish throat sound from a milkman. Had he heard right? The tooth dripped venom into his red lacquer throat, glands swelling like a great egg. Seeing his disbelief, the milkman pulled aside his jacket, undid the belt of his trousers. He unbuttoned his pants, pulled one side of his trousers down until he had exposed his bright white buttock. Snow fell on a black brand mark, an acute angle, forty-five degrees, one centimeter to the side, pointing down, a hand's width from his pinched rectum.

The unused blue lab coat still hung on a hook beside the quilted maroon robe. Eli's glass left a wet ring on Karl's *Kulturbund Performance Book* festooned with crooked crosses. Imperturbable, Karl hoisted on his heavy pack, angrily stuffed full by Vera while Eli (sea-lion face, gangrenous molar) mixed sand into paint. Eli had been engrossed by pigment and perpetual tooth pain for weeks. For once the word *pimf* had gone by with no remarks. Cardiac chiseling, insomnia, apprehension. Vera fried in margarine, chanced on a pompous recipe to distract from consequence piled on consequence. Into the margarine went bronzed potatoes after wooden turnips while Eli painted a red and black chalk map of Thailand with a horsehair brush. He trimmed the map with decorative pepper trees, pearls, tomatoes, a woman's legs in lilac shoes. Title: *Ici Repose*. Vera tidied, wiped crumbs on which black ants were attached and set down their plates.

You've strayed, she commented, noticing the chalk smudge.

He labeled the gateway, *Running Dog*, inserted a north/south arrow, while troubling thoughts persisted: Have we been shadowed? Could Karl…? Why those youth meetings? The neighbor's arrest? Who gave the tip? Eli watched his son wet, then comb, oily hair using the last drops of Vera's rose water.

Karl asked for salt but the ration was used up. His tiny eyes were monolithic while lingering on glaring spatial disharmonies in his father's map. Eli saw no seismic changes in those oblique eyes, just Karl refusing the unappetizing feast of green apples that had very little realizable sweetness.

Is there an egg? Is there soup?

Yes, there is lumpy but filling soup.

Horsemeat?

At seven hundred francs a kilo, don't make me laugh.

Eli ate with as little chewing as possible, as quickly as possible and climbed into the brass bed, pressing his suppurating cheek against Vera's pillow.

Rain squalls slammed the shutters like galloping horse hooves. A mongoose with oily hair, Eli narrowed his eyes. There were claw marks across his cheek, the building smelled of wet bedding and a backed-up toilet. He had no shirt collars left. Sonia Stern-Terk Delaunay and her husband Robert were gone from rue Saint-Simon to the Auvergne region. Or, perhaps, to Mougins? Or Grasse? Adolphe Féder, charged with harboring resisters, was locked up with his wife at Cherche-Midi prison. Or, at Drancy where Jacques Gotko surely was. Max, Isis, Moishe. Chaim was hidden in some ungodly place. What a mistake it was to leave wildflowers, cabbages and beets. What thirst. No exhibits for five years, youth past. Eli saw gloomy impasto and smeary surface. Acerbic Vera mended Karl's haversack. She kept two cigarettes for herself, rolled socks, smelled Eli's pus. The only penicillin to be had was on the black market and they had nothing left to sell. The gendarme warned of another air raid and there were snipers on the roves. There was no coal whatsoever while the cooking gas was turned on between seven and eight and twelve and one thirty only.

Vera's glasses magnified brown circles around her eyes. She tossed dead leaves from the cups, jabbed the needle into her bun, swallowed *du fea*, *de l'eau*, *de la terre*, *de l'air*, then carrots, turnips, barley coffee. Her owl-of-Minerva face remained inscrutable. Still hungry, she wrapped the bread for Karl's journey in used drawing paper. Their *kleinen buergerlichen* (petit bourgeois) stood before them with unalterable resolution wearing a macabre uniform, holding his rucksack at eye level asking for their bread. His voice was hard to hear over the exploding shells. His copper-colored eyes weren't curious. He sucked a fruit drop, smelled his mother's unwashed short-sleeved dress. He imagined her name and Eli's in the *Totenbuch* (deathbook).

Two adults between sixteen and forty-five = one French prisoner of war (1945). Their names would be deleted from the national register at the time of the exchange. Eli's tongue had gone white. Very soon after the train departed, a switch changed, shunting them south. It stopped in a railway yard, soon started again. They sat beside a village priest on a wooden plank gazing outside at mounds of brick and broken walls seeing plumes of black smoke rising up from prehistoric mounds.

Bend down! Eli requested.

He curled his hand into a scoop, cupped it against her pudendum. The priest ate artificial honey from a cardboard box, had turned his head away but not his eyes. There was a bag on the priest's lap, in it vestments and chalice, white cloth and candles. He took a keen interest in (it seemed to him) a donkey and a dog whose fucking was not interrupted by the umbrella or the sewing machine tumbling against them when the train screeched around a curve. *Tableaux sauvage* aside, Eli's legs bent with tumescent fervor while Vera's head (a red balloon) was thrown back. Her tiny breasts were pendulous, her propellers, sex and chute, looked like two red spinning holes while her dripping tongue was Prussian blue. To reach deeper, Eli's fat worm curled into a treble clef. The train wheels ground, cars crunched against each other, white antennae-like thread curled in arabesque against and punched through Vera's uterine pear. *Voilà.* The new *pipel*. Hatless. No black homburg. No turban. Conceived in delectation.

THE ONION FRATERNITY

Lonelier than usual, Ira laid down the gaunt-
let, rested his head on Eli's shoulder. Interminably
prone, Eli's profile in death pose was noncommittal.
His face rose above the beaver-trimmed spread as a
long apron of silence (not fraught) brewed an African
shield above father and son. Vera's telephone rang,
her adding machine crocheted. The dachshunds ate
liver-flavored prisms in the kitchen and her noodles
knelt piously on the kitchen table, casting shadows.
The noodles had already been kneaded, then rolled
into a floury coil and sliced. After smoking a cigarette she spread the slices and left them to dry on a
clean cloth and crept into the bedroom to check on
Ira. She placed her palm of concern across his forehead, felt for a fever, felt none. She rolled an orange
across the piano keys, kissed Ira on the head, told
him, Listen, Fuzzball, it's Debussy.

She demanded, Get up. Get better. You've wasted
the day.

Vera puffed up the emerald-green pillowcase under Eli's neck.

Who is Fiescher? asked Ira. Who is Aletsch? Who is Pyla?

Ira wanted to get up but didn't want to wear the carpet slippers left on the chair, soles up, to ward off bad luck. He didn't want to wear pajama bottoms, refused to join the onion fraternity.

Stop calling me Fuzzball!

Brown crew cut stood up stiff on his scalp. If Eli was dead, as it seemed, why was Vera carrying in the revolving easel? If Eli could work and sleep in Jockey shorts, didn't have to wear pajamas, could walk barefoot, why couldn't he? Flies dozed in the air above Eli's open mouth, his smelly breath a billow of sulfur and chlorine. There were two empty bottles of peppermint liquor drunk with Fiescher, Alitsch and Pyla until dawn upright on the windowsill, also wet cigar ends. An influx of fish stink steeped the bedroom. Ira knew the smell – sardines. He heard the clink of tin hitting garbage can, smelled scorched toast. Ira held back piss, studied the chestnut wallpaper's yellow trim: Big flower. Little flower. Medium flower. Man carrying a rock. He weighed the comestibility of Eli's ring with its milky succulent jewel, tried to bite it off Eli's hand, but the jewel wouldn't budge. He let his father's hand drop back onto the spread as though it had no bones and didn't need to obey gravity.

For the third time the phonograph played *You Make Me Feel So Young*, sung by Frank Sinatra. Vera worked, hummed along, …*there are songs to be sung*. She couldn't complain. She was complete with man, child, home, allotments. She reached for her *brif-shteller* (letter-composer) preparing to approach another gallery, hat in hand. Eli's Vera: Not young but not old, shelterer of Eli, eavesdropper with conch ears. Her neck was stretched to get ahead, the never-silent bell, her mouth, remained pert. She wore short sleeves because her arms were unfailing potent sources of Eli's desire. She wrote a begging letter, eyes lowered, folded it and addressed an envelope, licked a minty stamp. Business obtruded, observance to money making, accounts columns, ledgers. Vera knew very well one coin from the next. She had a drawer for small cash, another for incoming. She thought, Just like Mama, I eat leftovers too. I never sit down, eat in haste, I slap and scold, pawn pearls. *I kill myself for you*, Mama told us every day. Finally I know what she meant.

Vera shouted, Ira, your pajamas! Your slippers, please.

She regretted the harsh sound of her voice, lowered it, Marigold, please.

Vera worked in Doric columns on eggshell sheets: <u>Current</u>. <u>Deposits</u>. <u>Reckoning</u>. <u>On Account</u>. Her clients were objects of Eli's derision though they stood waist high in a red carnation field of debt. She sharpened yolk-yellow pencils, used a soap eraser, brushed the specks (black as crushed olive pits) away with the back of her hand. "Party Line" (the saber wit of Elsa Maxwell's gossip), coated the background. Lupine and wild poppies drooped in a glass on her desk, beside them, her trusty wooden ruler with its metal straight edge. On the sheet in front of her, lines of numbers, a display of fireworks. Her clients provided their entire income. As always when lost in fives, nines and fours, her spine sagged and she'd hear Mama's voice speak derisively: *Hände auf den Tisch*. At that, she'd put her palms down on the desk, would breathe in, resharpen a pencil to a needle point. 2.80 + 4.30 + 26.80 + 42.30 + 51.60 + 2.30 + 1.30 + 1.30 + 19.80. Numbered bricks, a wall of money.

Vera carried in the blue china tray, laid it on the eiderdown and left the room. There were sardines mashed with a fork on toast, a meal Ira hated, but because Vera and Eli liked sardines, Vera had cornered the supply. Ira glared at the tray.

You have gall to prepare mud for me when I'm sick. You know I hate sardines!

This meal, when seen by polar projection, glowed. To Ira it looked like mud on toast. On the tray also, a jelly glass of bright orange Tang.

Mommy, Is Daddy dead?

Ha.

Vera dropped a fresh deck of playing cards on the tray, spilled salt.

Play cards. Spare me a battlefield.

She cast Eli a china look and left the room. Ira pushed the tray across the eiderdown so he could remove ace to ten from the deck, all diamonds and arrange them left to right – seven, five, two eight, six, three, ace, ten, nine, four. He picked up all ten cards and turned them face downward, held the little package in his hand as if about to deal. Said, out loud, A.

He slid one card off the top of the pack and placed it at the bottom. Said, C. He placed the next card underneath, said, E, placed another card underneath. Said, Ace.

He turned the next card face up on the bed. An ace, he announced, sliding the next card off the top of the packet, placing it at the bottom of the deck. He said, W, placed this underneath,

O, placed it underneath.

He turned a card face up. It was a deuce. No fun, he thought, No audience. I'm not Daddy, not sardonic, not an ironist. He rubbed his eye. Mischance made me. I was born a chatelaine, not like Karl, the rooster, who ruled the roost. The cards were yellow and gray with inedible pink designs. Ira was hungry but never for mashed sardines. He gave a sidelong look at (undeodorized) Eli, the cartographer, again studied the wallpaper trim: Big flower. Little flower. Medium flower. Man carrying a rock.

I'll starve to death! he warned with a tremulous voice to deaf ears.

He could hear Vera's business voice on the telephone but not what she said. His ears of corn were the problem, they were filled with fluid.

Mam Meh, the words jumped.

Vera could lean over her plinth desk for seven days in a row and work while Ira sat watching the wonder box nursing a grudge against Eli who spoke with an accent and got up as late as he liked.

Marigold, Vera shouted, Get out of bed, stretch your legs.

Ira harbored a litany of grudges. He made a list:

Ma's cigarette smoke chokes me.

There are two boxes of cigarettes in her bathrobe pocket.

She drinks bitter black coffee, leaves lipstick on the cup.

I have a two-way wrist watch radio from Dick Tracy comics but no one—brother, sister, father, mother, friend, rabbi, priest—who'll watch my card tricks.

Vera's wisecracks.

Eli's Jack Benny imitations.

Vera's crumby eyeglasses from the peddler who keeps a mirror attached to a stick, doesn't speak any language known to man.

Ira willed a new mood. He kicked the brass back of the bed. Clank. Propped up by pillows, he opened his mouth for cherry syrup, slurped one teaspoonful, swallowed it, dribbled onto the eiderdown. He noticed a bubble of spit at Eli's lips. Eli opened his amber eyes.

I'm thirsty.

His head shook.

It wasn't my fault, Ira told him, indicating the cherry drips.

Woodpecker pecks started up. Eli reached for and swallowed the liquid in the glass on the tray.

I'll skin you alive if you fail your logarithms, were the next words out of Eli's mouth.

Eli's face was damp, his mouth full of coated teeth, coated partial bridge, a ferocious boar's snout. There were pieces of canvas in haphazard piles. The paintings were commemoratives: Botanical gardens on Long Island. Gloster, Mississippi. Sacred Grove of Bialowiezca. Boulevards of Flushing. All were maps in some form or other, oozing high spirits, including addled images and brash colors. Above the closet door, on Vera's side of the bed, a minute map called *Red Handkerchiefs of the Hietzing District, Bundesgymnasium, Wien XIII.* Eli set down the empty Tang glass. Acids curdled his stomach.

You von't forsake me, vill you, kid?

Eli took up the plate, mashed the sardines into paste, made crisscrosses with the fork. In two bites one slice was gone, in two more the other. Now Ira wanted the toast, even the mash of sardines, now he was not just hungry, was ravenous.

You stink, he spat at his father.

Eli laughed so suddenly that tears poured down. Ira rolled over onto his stomach so he could kick Eli in the hairy ribs with spongy heels, making Eli laugh so hard again that Vera came to the doorway to see what was so funny.

Vera kicked her two dachshunds outside the kitchen, touched the floury coil resting on the clean cloth braided into twists. She turned on the oven, pinched off a bit of dough.

Take this.

She dropped it into her son's guppy and goldfish bowl before sliding the loaf into the oven. Done. She smoothed eraser flecks from her cotton dress, covered her eyes with both hands, stood at the window watching through her fingers as the dachshunds romped across the yard, pissing on the plaster gnome. Unscrewing a jar of gherkin pickles, she ate two standing up, stuck a fork into an Oscar sardine and poured the leftover oil down the drain. She thought, Open the prison. Turning on the tap she washed utensils in the sink. When the time came to remove the bread from the stove and glaze it with egg white, she laid a chartreuse-plaid dishtowel over it. Nothing left but to face Eli. Difficult to. Difficult not to. Last night's lust ungratified, the days before, too infrequent, not embued with idiosyncrasy. No astringency anymore, merely a metronomic pumping insertion, a museum of extracted teeth. Vera glanced out the window in time to see rocks tumbling across the yard. Quickly, she opened the screen so the dachshunds could lumber inside before closing it against the rockslide, against all authority. Rose and beige light tumbled through the silvery screen into the kitchen, across the floor, across the face of the snow owl clock. Herringbone shadows found the bread that had begun to smell up the room. With a sharp fingernail, she scratched a white line along her wrist toward her palm.

Brushing together the crumbs from inside the cream-and-red breadbox, she trapped them with four fingers, pressed them into her mouth. She was weak-kneed, horny again. Without provocation, the cold water tap turned counterclockwise, emitted a squeal. Her thoughts: Roast chicken for tomorrow's meal? Or cutlets? The faucet dripped perfectly formed golden tears of melted butter. Must steam and iron Eli's dinner jacket. Barbarous Eli. When he talks, I listen; when he sleeps, I am quiet. The yoke of... Gallstones... How to get rid of Jesus. Get back into bed with Moses while the macaroni is boiling.

✦

The smell of roasting chicken steeped everything. Eli's easel leaned against the bed. Close by, Ira sat on the window ledge, fuzzy-brained, his back to Eli, laundering sour envy, listening to the lob-scratch-suck of paint.

Eli mumbled, Fresh *babka*, not chicken.

Uxorious father, salt of stupidity, eclogue in wooden shoes. Ira made a fig gesture at his back.

Vera admitted her garden through the window. It was well-stocked with colossi, peppers, blackberries, tumbledown vines, cat-like faces of young sunflowers, foxish Philcos, seedlings sprayed for aphids. The yard was screened to keep out deer, fox, nomads, Arabs. Eli had mixed volcanic ash from Mount Sinai in with the fertilizer. Gathered in one corner were raked cauliflowers, potatoes, one tree with umbrella boughs, a railroad timetable tacked to its trunk. Orange nasturtiums climbed up the bark and tangled around the flat white thumbtack that held the timetable. Eli's smell was sour but also sweet. Turpentine vapor stung Ira's eyes though he liked the squeezed-worm smell that lingered all day. Eli, devil-may-care, stalked back and forth, auburn hanks of hair (like Julius Caesar's) across his forehead pate. Taste, distaste, cold color, hot color. Today's cartography: Flushing decorated with wide-brimmed velvet hats, top and bottom, fur hats left and right. Ira's back tensed, his fingers reordered the deck of cards by suit. His secret: He would worship Daddy if he could swallow the stuck pit. Karl.

Vera shouted, Ira, take off your dirty underpants, put on the pajamas.

She marched into the room.

Open wide, Eli.

Eli opened his mouth. He daubed paint while Vera brushed his coated teeth in rolling motion.

Put some lead in my pencil, Eli challenged her.

Now spit, she told him.

He spit into the soup bowl she held.

Symbols in pea green: Interstate highways, thick line completed, broken line, under construction. Symbols in mint green: Other highways, divided, paved, unpaved. Symbols in loden green: Connecting roads, paved or unpaved. China red: Principal through roads. Black crosses: No connection between roads. Scale: One centimeter equals 11.2 kilometers/1:1,200,000 had been written across the flaccid area with brown chalk. From a brown paper bag Eli snatched a handful of dried grasshoppers and popped them one by one into his mouth.

Stick out your tongue, Ira, his mother insisted.

He let her look at his tongue, whined, I'm starving to death.

He swallowed, was feeling better.

Okay, I'll put the wash on the line.

Eli popped a blue P in while his son's mouth was open.

Ira fastened a union pin to the lapel of his pajama top, put on the bottoms and flicked his fingers until an electrical current shot out. He was content, read *Arabian Nights* all afternoon. At one point he asked, Daddy, is it true that the king raped a virgin every night for one thousand and one nights? Is it true that the king had her beheaded at daybreak? Is it true that the king and Scheherazade lived forever?

Eli answered, Yes yes yes.

Ira's eyes went wherever Eli went.

Eli asked him, Shall we send your mother out for a quart of ice cream? Or, a quart of atoms?

The boy could almost taste the blinking, blue atoms, rife with flavor. Although he was fearful of the pull and squeeze of spaghettifaction, his mouth watered. But, he wondered, Is Daddy goading me? Nibbling from a cardboard box brimming with almonds and raisins, he had no doubt that if he was caught eating before supper, Vera would murder him in bed. His neck hunched into his pajama top like a turtle when the clock hammer struck six times. In the kitchen, Vera's feet moved like a goose's feet or the feet of a water carrier.

Of course she'll bring us dinner, Eli told him, Maybe fresh mice or duck liver. Maybe a red squirrel gripped in her talons along with figs that are fat and purple outside and milky inside...

Eli waxed on, ...*La menthe et le thym* (mint and thyme), and handed Ira a bag of Cheetos.

This boy's chin is like hers. The other had my chin. On the night table, Eli's blue bottle of Milk of Magnesia and Vera's carton of Salem cigarettes. At the foot of the bed, a crib filled with newspapers and crumpled Salem packs and corks.

The last light of day filtered onto the gladiolus along the eastern wall. Shallow breather that Eli was, Ira barely breathed at all. Eli's brown-stained fingers held a wine glass coated on the inside with liquid pink chalk.

I'm starving, Daddy.

One by one Ira folded the pages of *Arabian Nights* so that when he stood the book upright the pages turned by themselves like a windmill. The ear pain returned, he moaned.

Eli looked up. *Gazunt,* Ira.

He set his glass down and poured a spoonful of raspberry syrup into a flatware spoon, aiming it in the direction of his son's mouth. Ira shook his soft head.

No.

Eli jammed the spoon between his lips anyway.

It's this or the enema woman with her calf's bladder who'll aim her goose quill like I got when I was your age. Or, worse still, castor oil.

Ira's mouth dropped open. You said you were never a boy. You said you didn't have a mom, or a daddy either. If you were one, what did you do?

I spun my *dreidl,* trained white mice.

Ira pressed his arms around the hunger pang. Spun what?

My top.

What did you eat when you were a kid?

Eli picked up a palette knife and scraped off thick smears of paint from canvas.

I ate carnivores.

Scrape.

Rodents.

Scrape.

Shellfish.

Scrape.

Eaters of carrion.

Scrape.

Reptiles.

Scrape.

He hissed like a snake when Vera noisily swooped in, red wings beating and stirring the air.

Eli added, his voice cruel, I even ate birds of prey.

He didn't utter one word more but wound his arms around Vera's red wings until they were still, then kissed her hard beak.

Ira turned his nose up at the fifteen-cent Atomic Bomb Burger from the Tudor Grill. He was blue because Joe Louis (sad day in 1949) had been KO'd by Rocky Marciano. To cheer him up Vera sprinkled coarse salt onto the burger. One dachshund lifted his leg on the table leg. Vera smacked its rump and dropped a slim dinner mint onto the salt. Ira took big bites, fending off the dog.

Don't gulp, she snapped. Here's your legacy.

She clasped his cheek between two fingers, pinched so hard that tears sprang into his eyes. For supper she served potatoes and onions to Eli and vodka from a red-labeled bottle. Also for Eli: *Varenikes* (Ukrainian dumplings). Vera poured ground gunpowder into the pewter bowl beside the new citrine penknife for slicing green apples. Ira's fingertips twisted the end of his rope. When he ate on an empty stomach, enfeebled by hunger, there was no escaping the blown bugle of digestive juices. In front of him loomed the emerald city of Eli's map, keyed with small bats, bees and moths as well as other quaint symbols sprinkled across level terrain beside small hills and on lowlands.

Ira's eyes ran. He felt dizzy and fought back tears not from cheek pinching but for Joe Louis, a tower of muscle and butter, for whom he had (secretly) prayed. He'd begged: God. Let Joe Lewis win like you split the Red Sea. He had pressed his hands together, bowed his head, his fingertips touching the tip of his nose like he'd seen in *The Nun's Story* and …Here's the church, here's the steeple, open the door, see all the people. He wanted to sink into the ground when Eli materialized behind him, accused him (in his most mocking voice), Are you praying? Ira's hands had dropped apart as if caught stealing or touching himself. I hope you won't become a slave of the Pharaoh, Eli warned.

At the next fight, Ira swallowed a throat full of shame. Sulfur seeped up from cracks between pine floor planks and mixed with the smell of Joe Louis' fiery sweat. The pus from Joe's eye wound stank like cheese. Standing on tip-toe, Ira waved a red handkerchief fiercely, flexing prayer in his forearms. His scrotum squeezed to refute each pound on Joe's face until Joe crumpled and Ira let his soul shoot out to enter Joe who got up, punched but lost the fight.

Ira continued to smell him. He hadn't trimmed the shrubs that bordered the sun-soaked garden over which humming wasps and bees and various monotonous insects hovered. After the fight, Ira didn't feel his soul slip back. So much for prayer to Romeo (God) the wearer of fur.

Vera refilled his cocoa cup halfway up. Drink, she told him.

Ira zipped up his hooded mouse-skin jacket after Vera dropped another Atomic Bomb Burger onto the plate. Swishing her taffeta skirt, she dribbled honey, sprinkled fresh gray gunpowder.

Please trim the shrubs? she pleaded, Please.

His look said, Make me. Eli wiped kerosene-soaked brushes across the *Post*. Out of the blue he invited Ira, Come to the track! Do the shrubs later. Bat your eyes, Zorro.

At this, Ira swallowed the final bite, sucked his sweet/tart fingertips. He licked truculent lips and stood on the bed, sinking ankle-deep into feather bedding. Using the armchair as a bridge, he jumped across and broke off a twig from the lime tree.

Can we eat at the Automat?

Vera snapped on pearl earrings, pulled her hair back with a black ribbon. She had four petticoats under her flaired skirt. She folded the eiderdown back in order to air the sheets.

Why not, she answered.

That eiderdown (Eli's) came from world to world bundled up, filled with cabbage rolls, letters, tied with rope. It came away from the unnamed, unmentioned village (settlement) where the snow was so deep it reached the roof, where the single window frosted over. During a cold Easter after Eli had gone, his Zaida, was stalked and bludgeoned for sport, hadn't defended himself but sank into knee-deep snow and was dropped into a frozen well, poisoning it for the spring thaw, causing the village to blame him and his many remaining children. Inside that hut (hovel) twigs were piled to the ceiling. Amber beads were used in lieu of coins and stuffed into the eldest (there were five) sister's stocking. Talking twilight moldered all day except for a red glow at dawn. Little else but soup or groats (not both) was eaten with too much pepper and too much salt, sometimes bread with chicory. On the table next to the spice box, a stack of sorrel leaves. The sounds there: A hammer hitting an anvil, frogs, crickets, growls of starved dogs, feet shuffling on the dirt floor, *Oy vey* resounding from under Mama's kerchief like it did when she bent to fold the eiderdown into the wicker trunk for Eli to take away. That day tears soaked the goose feathers. More fell when she bent over to scour a pot with sand. But, she said nothing, just sloshed boiling water from side to side in the pot. The stink of *gefilte* fish for the special occasion lingered. Her (also silent) husband made the blessing. Neither made eye contact with the youngest (of four) son, the one going away, or with any of their children. Papa was just back from the tavern after sixteen hours of refilling and watering glasses with vodka that the travail-free drunkards drank and drank and drank.

Eli sat in the bathtub drinking a bull shot while shampooing his hair to celebrate the burst boil seething with ants. He brushed a pink plastic (Swedish) nail-brush vigorously across encrusted nails, rubbed various body parts with a wash cloth while singing *Life with an Idiot* in falsetto voice. Waiting, Ira was dressed in a pillbox hat, its strap under his large chin. He wore skin-tight trousers with festive silver braids along both legs and sleeves of the purple Tyrolean suit. Vera handed Ira a blue enamel cup filled with juice.

You smell like rotten shellfish, she told him.

Can she possibly smell it? Ira wondered.

Eli stepped from the bath. He had hair along his spine, was lobster pink. Vera sprinkled talcum powder back and front.

You smell like shrimp cocktail, Eli commented, pulling off the hat and tousling Ira's pompadour for luck, then dousing his own hair with Vitalis. He joked, Oyster-eater, bear with a sore head.

Dad must know. But how would he know?

Vera heard the kettle whistle. It disfigured the quiet. Lime-lit, the hot steam trickled through the house, opening Ira's ears and nose. At last he breathed. How can they smell absolutely everything? They are the smell police. The peacock-blue, aphrodisiac steam gave Ira the urge to go back inside, barricade the door, fill his hand with petroleum jelly, and rub himself again.

✦

His parents drank milk from tins – thick, sweet evaporated milk. Columns of Pontiacs and Chevys and Fords passed the house, blue as olives, even before rose streaks exhaled across the horizon. Vera gathered her Nordic knot of resilient hair at the nape of her neck. On Sunday she served mint sorbet, an omelet garlanded with wild figs along with cherubs in sea shells to husband and son.

Genocide Mom, Ira quaked, drenched from a downpour.

The day was short (*rasputitsa*), the ground covered with snow, the river frozen. Wrapped in her pink quilted robe, Vera added rice and too much salt to water, said nothing. Eli said nothing. Ira was sweaty with f.o.i.d. (fear of impending doom) again. In order to fend off a possible nuclear attack he walked in four circles, clapped his hands eleven times.

Is the door locked? he asked in panic. What about the KKK? he queried with alarm.

Vera and Eli locked eyes.

Enough Job, enough.

Then we're safe?

How can we promise you? How are we to know? his father shrugged.

Vera harrumphed, asked, Why quit? Halvah doesn't quit. Did Matisse quit? He worked hard, like Daddy works.

Ira paced along the narrow ledge (*urime yidn*). He didn't care what she said, he was quitting the club. He wondered, Am I a heron, an apostle, a Salvationist? Should I be like Bergman chasing tigers with binoculars, traveling under leafy trees along forked roads with an unprotected scrotum? He gazed at the punch lines of jokes he'd encoded on an index card:

I got fifty bucks that says he's dead.
You're lucky that you're not a herring.
Fine. Common or preferred?
He falls, she falls, Niagara Falls.
Shell them, of course.
Needs salt.

Ira practiced, Shell them, of course, and returned the index card to his wallet.

In Vera's black leather purse: toenail scissors, tweezers, magnifying mirror, bag of jewelry the size and weight of a brick, Chesterfield/soft pack, Zippo lighter, sticks of Blackjack gum. While Ira listened to his parents' lunching/whispering/cooing, he reached inside Vera's purse and removed three bills, two coins. He thought twice, returned one bill but took more coins. These coins were hot. He hid a bill inside the rubber-banded box that contained baby hair. What Vera's glossy black sealskin coat meant to her, those ringlets of gold meant to Ira. He put the cash into his pocket. They could buy: Dubble Bubble Gum to chew in wads in the infield where he always stood (feet splayed) ready to charge in or back away at a clip, anticipating sun-dapple so blinding he would miss the high fly. The bill could go toward: A portable radio. A (secret) crucifix on a chain with the lank figure of J.C. dangling from it. Tony Modliani, Ira's best friend, went to St. Anne's Catholic School, wore a school uniform and kept such a crucifix in his pocket. Tony would cross himself when their bus passed a Catholic church. He explained to Ira how he went down on his knees in church, had his knuckles rapped by a nun and when and how he touched the crucifix to his lips. Ira longed for a bleeding/suffering Christ to touch to *his* lips too. He craved the putrid kiss of Jesus. Ira checked his face in the mirror for signs of guilt, saw a telltale smirk adhering to the corners of his mouth. He pulled an old flesh-colored wad of gum off the side of the radiator and dropped it between his lips, spat the attached paint chip across the room. The gum was hard as tire rubber. He worked his jaw in grinding motion. It was flavorless, like old rubber cement, another non-edible he often chewed despite its chemical taste. The effort on his jaw eased away the famous guilty smirk. He charged through the kitchen while buttoning his jacket.

Vera yelled, Do you need money?

He locked eyes with the stinking Puss'n Boots cat food can on top of the garbage.

Yes.

She dropped a dime onto his outstretched hand. Eli's voice came from nowhere, Thank Mama.

Thanks, Mom.

Vera got shrill, Kiss Papa before you go.

He pretended not to hear.

Eli's words were repeated, Thank Mama.

I did!

Then he saw Eli with his back against the doorway and Eli mocked, Irish buttonhole!

This meant that his chinos were tucked into the crevice between the cheeks of his ass, so, he grabbed a fistful of cloth, tugged it from between his cheeks, banged the screen door so hard it flew back open.

He traveled by Schwinn to Tony's across the schoolyard, cutting through an empty lot, past Carvel, past Carolee's brick apartment building, through another empty lot to Tony's attached house. Tony Modliani's father drove a Dugan's Bakery truck delivering bread and icing-covered cupcakes door-to-door. When Mr. Modliani wasn't working, the bread truck was parked in front. Embarrassed or not, Tony got driven to the movies in it.

Tony asked Ira, How much you got?

One twenty-five. You?

Twenty cents.

They pooled the coins on Tony's palm: one dollar, one dime, six nickels, five pennies. A new holy card of a barefoot shepherd holding a staff was pinned onto the bulletin board. Above the shepherd's head, a green egg-shaped aura (halo?) also, a green blanket was draped over the shepherd's shoulders. *"St. Jude, Apostle, martyr and relative of our Lord, intercede for us. To be said in cases despaired of."* The saint was shoeless. They stood over Tony's fish tank. In it swam two narrow silver-brown speckled piranhas.

Tony egged on Ira, You're too chicken to stick your dangler in.

Ira squinted at the little faces reputed to be able to strip flesh to the bone with their razor teeth.

You are chicken shi --

Before he heard the "t" in "shit," Ira dropped his chinos and Jockey shorts and bent across the tank, his Caucasian-pink dangler shrunk like a radish. It didn't reach water, but, as he strained, the ribs pressed against his lungs. Ira grunted at the sharp teeth in a row, the triangular blades. He saw points of a king's crown razor (tangerine and cobalt) in the tank light. Ira conjured the piranha's jaw stripping his non-foreskin faster than the speed of light. A cooked sheep, he thought, Alone on a white tablecloth, no help from the loaves, from the wine, the cake, the fishes.

No! he croaked, changing his mind, pulling at the elastic until his Jockeys were almost up to his armpits.

Confidently he explained to Tony: When a man and a woman are on their backs, the woman on top of the naked man, head to foot with her legs under the man's arms, the dangler attaches to her navel. Seeds shoot from his garden to hers. A baby is planted in her dirt.

Cranberry shapes appeared on Tony's face. Ira had done it again. Tony would have to tell *all* in confession. Ira always made trouble but gravity pulled them together. Also: Wildroot Cream-Oil, Joe Louis, unshined shoes, Mounds Bars, one lunar eclipse. (On that unforgotten night the moon had risen above the horizon when the earth passed between the sun and moon. Tony and Ira watched for the shadow cast onto the moon through dark colored glass. Afterwards: macaroons and sliced peaches.)

Sleep over, Ira? invited Tony.

Nah. Ma said, Sleep in your own bed.

So ask your Dad, he's a soft touch.

Nah. He's mad that I didn't speak nice enough to Ma.

Will you help me with my homework?

What's your problem?

A man six feet tall stands at a distance of ten feet from a lamppost. The lamp is twelve feet above the ground. How long will the man's shadow be?

Ira didn't have to think.

I don't know. What's your next problem?

There are two railway stations, A and B. They are connected by a single track line. Owing to some mistake, a train leaves A for B at the same time as another train leaves B for A.

Are there safety devices?

No. No signals either.

There'll be a collision.

Is it true that a minus sign turns everything upside down, like the reflections of trees and houses in a river?

True. It's true.

Thanks, Ira.

Two out of three – fountain of cypress. Ira unbuckled and re-buckled his belt, up one notch. He re-tucked his graphite-gray shirt that happened to be the same color as Tony's hopping and chirping bird. Passing through the living room, was Tony's father (Sal) asleep on the living room couch covered with a tartan wool blanket. He was a taxi driver on weekend nights. Shiny bristles gleamed across his lip and chin, a sand-colored poplin jacket hung on the back of the nearby chair, its pockets full of last night's tips. As he passed by, Tony dipped his finger into the jacket pocket, took two quarters, did a little fox trot. Following at his heal, Ira reached in too, scooped a handful of change, so many dimes and quarters, a pirate's treasure. He did a Lindy but lost his balance and splayed the coins across the room. Crawling along the floor to retrieve them, Ira returning most to the jacket pocket. Tip-toeing, they got outside without waking Sal. Ira handed Tony five quarters, one dime.

Tony told Ira, I'll burn in hell.

Will I? asked Ira.

You're not Catholic.

Who will know?

God.

How?

God can see everything.

Even into the bathroom? How?

Tony shook his head yes. Ira couldn't imagine how, though he had observed something grow from nothing in a glass Petri dish, something that looked like snippets of fur or a piece of pink bologna shaped like a cloud with the texture of human tongue or green mold on Wonder Bread or a scab. Am I being looked at in the toilet? he wondered in panic.

✦

Sitting on the curb counting cars, waiting for Tony, Ira chewed on an approbation sandwich. His thought, in fragments: ... don't mimic me ... a rebuff ... a wise guy ... so what if I'm thoughtless? ... brown and white ... a dollar ten. He swore up and down that he was undervalued. He hated Vera's hair, had stomach kinks, had just refused the dinner of fish sticks. First, a hunger strike, now a big appetite. He listed complaints:

I hate lousy women drivers
my joke's a flop
I don't feel like running to the store
my ass is too big
my shoulders are narrow
my sneakers smell bad

The friends ate with Eli and Vera. Ira cringed while Eli gnawed a stinky raw onion. Vera's dachshunds slept under the table. When Vera struck wooden matches to light the gas range, the sticks broke in two. Tony refused herring in cream so Vera served him a kind of soft bread he'd never seen before smeared with golden chicken fat while she heated tomato soup in a Pyrex saucepan. Crumbs dropped onto Tony's maroon-and-blue striped polo shirt. Tony froze when Eli noisily drained a Rheingold can and crushed it in his sickle hand.

Vera asked Tony, Are you ill at ease?

Ira interjected, How quick is quicksand? Could the Titanic have sunk in quicksand? Could I sink into quicksand?

A yellow light bulb burned, snow bulbs sprouted in a bowl of bone-bleached pebbles. Vera reached for a plump fruit from a bowl, smiled as Eli unknotted his cravat, his spirit flagging under a long, gray winter smelling of dead earth.

Tony told Mr. and Mrs. G, My parents bought an almost new Philco. We jewed them down until they sold at Father's price.

A hair caught in Ira's throat. He twisted the sleeve of his striped polo shirt, watched Eli open another can of beer. Eli hollered, Lower the flame.

Vera lowered the flame, poured the soup, filled cups to the brim unaware that the tip of her silk scarf had dangled into the saucepan. She mopped a swatch of tomato soup across Tony's crew cut while turning to serve Eli. Impassive, Ira ate everything in sight: Herring, tomato soup, six White Castle hamburgers with dime-sized pickles, dollops of ketchup, grilled/chopped onions, a Devil Dog in one go. Conversation left the room. Glowing gas escaped from Ira's ass, formed an aurora borealis of orange ice-mist and hung like a cloud above him. Delicate icicles squeezed from nothing. Tony reached up, broke one off, gaily dropped it down the back of Ira's polo shirt. Vera complained that her litigation never came to an end and kept her connected to the long gray scar that got white from nerves and cold. When the phone rang, it was her lawyer. She talked though clenched teeth. One time Ira had asked about the scar, Eli had waved him away, scoffed, A beetle in a carnation. Don't listen to him. Vera had scoffed back, Put an eyedropper full of vinegar under the beetle shell, that will take care of that. You'll see.

In profile Tony and Ira were the same. They gaped at Eli after he changed into a tuxedo and tried on Vera's long evening gloves. Vera served cranberry juice in Sau-Sea Shrimp Cocktail glasses. Her son stamped his foot. I hate cranberry. How many times do I have to remind you? Let's get out of here, he ordered Tony.

Tony shrugged at Mr. G., passed through the doorway just before his best friend slammed the door behind them.

You forgot your mitt, Tony whispered, afraid to say more, as he lifted the bike lying on its side.

They pedaled under a canopy of tulip tree crowns, like inverted cones providing dense shade and towering over young (golden) birches, blazing maples, red dogwood and sumac. Not systematic, but pedaling alongside each other beside the white and blue Nile. Ira smoked a mentholated Kool. When his head brushed low hanging leaves a pair of birds rose up, flapped their wings, made indignant squeaks. They dropped their Schwinns on a mound of brown leaves and crossed chaparral by foot to a tree beside a lake. Above them on a limb, two long-necked birds groomed each other. Elsewhere in the tree, a lone bird that had a black cap spread its wings, cocked its head from side to side and bounced up and down, singing a vibrating trill. This bird had a white face, an orange and lemon bill, long tufts of yellow hair streamed down its back from the rear of its red-ringed eyes.

Ever unsatisfied, Ira followed Tony with his eyes while Tony gathered tinder and dry kindling. They created a nest upon which to layer wood in log cabin fashion. Ira lit the nest using a match from a *Copacabana* matchbook that was festooned with leopard stripes stolen from Vera's purse. Tony gathered more kindling while Ira fed the weak flame with dry castor oil plants. They witnessed a commotion when a bird with a red gular patch (the size of a small balloon) landed on a strong branch directly overhead. They felt sick at the sight of a twig drenched with saliva and charcoal hanging in its beak. The bird beat its beak against the branch until another like it landed and laid an egg. Finally, the fire took. Ira skimmed the surface of the lake with their metal bucket gathering green shapes decorated with red dots. He waded into the water up to his knees, soaked his chlamys, shoes, socks, chinos, saw colorless foam floating past and scooped half a bucketful, carried it ashore. He went down on his knees in the dirt. In the bucket, beneath the foam, were gray, guppy-like creatures whose long tails trailed behind. Several had two heads, a few were oddly shaped like human thumbs with frog eyes. Distracted by the bird with the crimson pouch, they saw the pouch fade to pale orange where it sat on its nest. Eyes locked to the bird, Tony stirred the bucket with a twig, blew on the fire. Hearing what sounded like a chisel, they gaped as a chick poked its head out of a crack in the shell. It was blind also covered in down and helpless (half in, half out of the broken eggshell), spotted with fly larvae. Ira pointed at the motley chick, made vomiting noises.

Miss Rheingold! he mocked.

Tony laughed and his face went (salamander-like) from red blotch to mustard.

Ira swung the bucket over his handlebar and ped-dled steadily, hardly sloshing, since he coped well with gravity. At Tony's house, they poured the gray guppies in with the piranhas. Ira's shirt was stuck to his back. Sweat had turned the collar copper-brown. Tony gave Ira's wrist an Indian burn, said, You're one of a kind, Ira. You eat faster than anyone I ever met. Your parents eat weird-like.

Weird?

Good weird. You never have chicken à la king, do you?

No, we don't.

You never get Kraft's macaroni or toasted Velveeta cheese on Wonder Bread?

I wish we did.

Tony turned off the basement lights and flipped a switch at the top of the tank.

It's ultraviolet light, invisible to the human eye, he explained.

The light revealed an emerald weave of curled DNA threading through the red glow of guppies with shimmering tails. Trails of yellow and green feces and urine crisscrossed like iridescent spun threads.

For Marilyn and Joltin' Joe! (1954) toasted Ira, an imagined glass in hand.

He picked up and petted Tony's mother's white Persian cat and pointed to a cluster of eggs at the bottom of the tank.

Do you begrudge him Marilyn? he asked Tony. I heard she eats prunes all day not to get fat.

Before Tony could reply, the overhead light went back on and the aquarium went dark. Tony's mother, Melba, marbleized. Her golden, shoulder-length hair reached the collar of her wrap-around robe.

She wore an amethyst ring on her pinkie. Ira could swear she had nothing on under the robe.

Studying? she asked, picking dried tomato soup off Tony with polished finger nails.

Little men, she cooed, It smells sour down here.

She unlocked the back door, propped it open with a cinder block and stepped outside to gaze at drifting red clouds. Back inside, she put her hand on Tony's throat.

You're burning up.

As she spoke, Tony began to shiver, couldn't swallow. Ira saw that his own hand was bluish and Melba was fading out of focus. Nauseated, clammy, he sat on the tan Castro.

They'll kill me, he told Melba who seemed like the woman whom Eli should have married.

Vera examined the raspberry rash encircling his ribs that itched like hell. She was wearing a brown suit with a high collar and ermine cuffs. She added fresh water to shriveled anemones in a small vase and touched his moist forehead with the palm of her hand.

Don't scratch. Stop scratching.

He couldn't stop. Flat in bed, he used a fork to get to an unreachable area of the lower back. Vera looked deeply into his retina for parasites, saw flickering diagrams, oscillating points of light.

I could kill you. She hollered into his ear.

Just like that. He didn't push her hand away, valiantly lay still while she tilted his head, held the eyelid open with two pincer fingers. He thought: I have no aunt to hide behind, no uncle to hitchhike to, no cousins, no priest, rabbi, pastor, postman, politician, crossing guard, plumber, bread truck driver, doctor, Joe Louis, Joe DiMaggio, no Ike, no protection against pinching fingers. When she released the eyelid, she stroked his damp hair. Eli's straight razor with the mother-of-pearl handle lay less than ten feet away. Vera could easily use it to kill him. Or, she could press the foam pillow in its white case over his face. I wouldn't last five minutes, my cheeks would implode, he realized. A dirigible of smoke rose from the long Chesterfield between her lips.

Ira bought time, begged, A glass of water, Ma. Pl…ease.

As she went to get the water, the taps on her shoes clicked against the black and white tiles. A straight razor across his throat would hurt like hell. He would be (as Eli would be) as pliable to a razor as a red poppy under the heal of her shoe. Wearing a surgeon's red rubber glove, Vera held the glass of water at eye level. Her long sigh did nothing to reassure him.

Drink it all.

He did. The worry abated though the fissure didn't close.

Ira, Why so much brittleness? Why so much rancor?

◆

A muggy day. He was coaxed to stay in bed by the ogre Vera who loomed over him holding a glass of milk. He felt wily and kissable, cheeky too, because yesterday he'd gotten his first blow-job parked in the ravine. When her mouth had opened, his eyes had grown into red rubies. Afterwards, his enormous thirst was quenched by Miller beer. He drank so fast it vomited itself back up along with a loud belch. The girl had moved back. She (the easy lay – t.e.l.) had seen him wearing white swim trunks with the blue stripes. Later, when he dropped her off at the A&P, she left her rosary on the seat of Eli's powder-blue Cadillac – a beaded chain with attached metal cross. She'd wrapped it around his tooled brown leather wallet. He licked around the half-healed fever sore. When they kissed, his tongue-tip had circled her bumpy tongue. Reviewing the event, he sat on the edge of the tub, the hair on his legs prickling like crabgrass because the fuse was lit. He could smell baking bread and coffee, spat into his hand. Rubbing spittle in clockwise motion, he saw torrential khaki and black spots. He lost touch, found touch, didn't smell bread any longer, just coffee.

Punch lines on the folded index card in his wallet:
Mr. Moskowitz looked up and said, Maybe a cookie?
Well then, said Abie, I definitely have shit in my pants
Beethoven's first movement
Pigmies are cunning runts
He's the one with whitewalls on his cement mixer

One who is two-and-a-half feet tall, has a ten-inch tongue, and can breathe through his ears

It keeps the pigeon shit off their lips

Give me a number quick, I gotta fart!

They both squirm when you eat them

Hold onto your nuts

Lying across the bed, black high-tops untied, he made an effort to memorize the punch lines. A good laugh: *Holy holy holy.* His biggest crime – a long face. He could imagine t.e.l. in a backless white dress while air blew up her skirt from a subway grate on which she was standing, legs wide, wearing white high-heeled shoes. Her flouncy pleated skirt might rise up, showing even the price tag on her white panties. Ira envisaged asking, What did the hurricane say to the coconut tree? What? He imagined her curiosity. He would make t.e.l. wait for his answer, would light a Kool and stare down her breasts (not of equal size), while languidly blowing smoke toward the ceiling. What? she'd ask again, dying to know. He'd put out the cigarette and tell her, Hold on to your nuts, this ain't going to be no ordinary blow job. He imagined her lipstick-smeared lips releasing mirth in a bubble. Ira scanned the index card for the next joke. Having examined the stretched pliable white cotton mound in her panties with his hand, he had found a fresh wet spot in the shape of a paramecium and had raised himself up on an elbow for a look. He'd seen that the wet spot was in the shape of a keyhole not a paramecium.

Eli was dressed up in a dark blue suit, a tie with plum polka dots and a button-down olive-drab shirt. When Ira showed him a photo in a men's magazine of a woman wearing a clinging, ruby-colored, sequined gown, Eli made no comment. Ira tried out a new joke: An American was surrounded by beautiful women on the beach. The Pollack was all alone. Excuse me, said the Pollack, How do you attract so many women? The American replied, I put a potato in my bathing suit, it drives women wild. The next week the Pollack saw the American again, grabbed him by the arm. You promised I'd drive women wild with a potato in my bathing suit! Look. I did what you said but women avoid me. The American looked, told him, Try putting it in the front.

Eli pulled at the end of his tie, asked, Are you done?

It's funny. Get it?

Eli opened his mouth so wide Ira could see where teeth were missing. He took his son's head, squeezed it in the crook of his arm like a nut-cracker.

You and your jokes.

What is a Pollack, Pop?

Eli massaged the nadir of Ira's skull. His brushes had been soaking all morning while he drew sheep and goats, manchineel trees with chalk. He needed to stretch canvases but had to show up at the I.N.S. wearing the tie, the camel-hair coat, the cashmere scarf.

Ira tried again. Why do Poles carry turd in their wallets?

Eli raised an eyelid.

Why?

For identification. Get it?

I get it. Ever meet a Pollack?

Ira shook his head.

Vera's voice came from her office, What do my little men want for lunch?

Renoir's three apples? Manet's four asparagus spears? Eli hollered back.

Her hair was piled (1959) on her pea head on which a tall honey-blond beehive was sprayed stiff as a bird's nest. She had little bird breasts, a strong heartbeat, a dwarfish trunk. Fire engine red lips pressed together with displeasure. First Ira's hand plunged down to her waist, then, his fingers crept another three inches, lying lightly on her butt, a pin-cushion. He had labeled her p.o.a (piece of ass).

P.o.a. told Ira, My father was killed in action in Korea. Don't grope me.

Although he was drenched in sweat, he no longer dared to mangle the springy butt or grab a handful of orange chiffon.

I wore this, she exclaimed, when I was bridesmaid for my mother when she married Dick.

Ira had no courage to subdue a girl whose father had gotten killed in a war, a girl who had just heated Campbell's tomato soup from a can and crumpled

Ritz crackers on top of it though she had pressed her nipples against his shirt buttons as soon as the soup can was tossed out.

There were blurred paw prints on the yellow kitchen linoleum. Blood flowed to his face when he bent to trim tough fungic toenails, letting the clippings drop on the floor. He tightened the drawstring on his madras pajama bottom while straining to bring up a big burp. His specialty, burps on demand.

Sweep them up, Vera hollered.

She halved deviled ham sandwiches, fretting to no one and everyone, It won't be enough?

Her glasses were mended with Scotch tape.

Chocolate or plain?

Chocolate.

As she rummaged through the refrigerator, Ira cadged three cigarettes from her soft pack of Lucky Strikes that leaned against the half-eaten goose crouched in gray juice astride a Pyrex pan.

I had the x-ray, she blurted out, filling a glass with milk, adding two spoonfuls of Nestlé Quik.

Ira made eye contact with the scar tissue along her forearm. Since she'd opened the refrigerator, the room was awash with a rotten smell.

Gross strawberries, Ira spat, They stink up the house. Must you buy them? Must you let them turn blue?

Vera smoothed the brown velvet negligee that hung snugly against her hips, ate a fat over-ripe strawberry, tossed the stem into the sink. The hurricane was beginning to whip toward them along the coast.

What about me? I'm hungry too, Ira reminded her.

She licked her lips that were thick with pale orange gloss. She hadn't kissed Ira's scornful cheeks since the night last summer when he'd gotten the fishhook caught in his eyelid. His face mouthed inaudible words of spite behind her back but no longer kissed, was unpredictable now. Ira wondered, Has Daddy noticed Ma's white pubic hair, right side only? If Ma died maybe Daddy should find someone who'd laugh at his jokes. Lauren Bacall? Susan Hayward? Simone Signoret? Natalie Wood? Maybe he'd find a chick who would drink straight-up gin martinis drink for drink with him, someone who wouldn't walk around half-undressed. Maybe someone with a pageboy who wouldn't turn everything around to make herself the center. Or, someone who didn't speak with a trip-up accent. Vera added coffee to her shopping list. On the list: cabbage, sweet peppers, capers, radishes, pears, lemons, beer, sour cream, carmine, ultramarine. The smoke from her cigarette formed a homey, rose-tinted cloud. Who was at fault? Money would help. Money, where did it go? More smoke shot out of her mouth in a cone. The window rattled from wind and rain. The darkened sky went from part-nocturnal to part-marine. Serving as a footstool, Vera knelt on one knee holding a tin of shoe

polish and a stained shammy cloth. She patted the
thin air above the shiny hollow moon knee.

Put it here.

Ira understood.

They smell bad, but they're cousins to the rose

He bent his knee, put his brown sockless loafer
with the polished Canadian penny in the slot onto
her knee.

The girl called it poison toadstool (p.t.), wouldn't
touch it unless he touched her. Ira was willing but
couldn't locate an opening. He patted the area, found
wool, then an outpouring of syrup. The hot syrup
dripped from somewhere. But where? Syrup conjured his scout leader, Mr. S., who had worn khaki
shorts with high brown socks, had a knobby Adam's
apple and a broom mustache. Mr. S. had instructed
the scouts in hot syrup making. Told them: Protect
your hands from drips. They're hot. Cook the sugar,
the butter and the corn syrup in the kettle, boys, stir
it with a whittled stick shaved of bark. Keep cooking,
boys, until a small drop hardens in well water. When
it's that hot, dip your apple-on-a-stick until it's coated. Twirl it in the air until it cools. If the corn syrup hardens before your candied apples are dipped,
boys, heat again, dip again but—a big but—keep
your hands away from hot drips. Ira poked around
her hot syrup from nowhere until he found where
nowhere was. She gasped. (Word unclear. Ouch?
Touch? Karl?) He removed his quim-coated hand

and darted into the bathroom to scrub with Ponds. Glimpsing his smirk in the mirror, he planted a lavish kiss on the cool glass, vowed an end to stinginess, a kick up his biology teacher's ass. He darted back and thrust his hand inside her panties once more. He had an hour until Vera returned from the doctor but an hour wasn't much.

You washed! she accused.

Don't hock me to China, he replied.

With the fingers of his right hand he plowed a furrow through her field, gazing over her head at a still life above the refrigerator – one onion veined by German rivers. Maybe he could make a film that started with her long legs, moved north, finally break in the movie camera given for his birthday. If he could, he would have close-ups only, black and white only. How else to expose starkness, coldness, loveless-ness? Before she left, Ira drew crumpled banknotes from his pocket for a tank of gas for her car.

✦

She asked, Why no foreskin?

He replied, A foreskin is redundant.

She asked, Do they tie the baby up in a receiving blanket? Are his legs tied down? Are his arms tied over the head? Is the individuality ignored? Are his limbs strained like Dürer men?

He replied, Don't ask me.

They drove along the Gulf, passed fishermen's nets made of chain mail. The setting sun jellied crevices and precipices beside the gravelly road. Ira sloughed off the mariachi music. Carmen bit into her apple like a capitalist. What would Joe Louis do with Carmen? What would Bergman do with the camera wrapped in burlap? What would Tony do with human skulls made of sugar? No gong rang. No round ended. No one sponged cold water onto his neck.

Unpropitious cathedral, Ira's hard head. She touched him with a splash of dash. His bedmate: Barbara, a Jewish temptress with changing Petri dish eyes, welded an acerbic tongue. At a roadhouse, Ira (a monkey's uncle) and Barbara (meddling, secretive) unrolled the wet map, unsure of the way. Unseasonal snow coated shocked oleander and chilled rose bushes. Barbara (140 pear-shaped pounds of ballast) had made a casserole with cubed bread crumbs, savory herbs, sautéed onions with butter, celery, mushrooms, broth, salt, pepper, celery seed, sage, rosemary, not a ton of fat for the journey. The smell visited the car while he built a case in his mind. How to tell her … There were blue-topped clouds above the historic marker: *Forty-nine steps to defilement.* Ira carried a sailor's duffel across his back. Inside it, film cans rattled against the green Prell jar.

He was asked, Eggs or cereal?

He tasted blood from bleeding gums. It was a riddle as to what instigated the bleeding, what nerve set it oozing, what biological substance was weeping? Barbara injected, Eggs, and added, What say an omelet of fast sperm? Why don't we do something to make up for the murdered millions?

Ira clamored across the mires and the puddles, his face into zephyr. Barbara tagged along. He'd folded the mettlesome conscription notice like a paper airplane and sent it for a ride. Airily, he tightened the belted raincoat. He got her to see *Love is Colder than Death* (1969) with him six times in New Orleans, was in love and in hate with Schygulla, with Fassbinder. Did the wild boar really live in a German forest?

Stagflation (1972), gloom of winter freeze. No dramatic focus after all. Barbara's tongue, a dull blade, Barbara's inhibition had escaped from its hiding places. She turned her wine glass upside down, put protein in the center of his plate but had no conscience about tossing the dishwater into the sparrow's nest. His retaliation was to harvest a crop of bravura and fertilize her bathwater. He brought two hand-stirred egg creams into the foggy bathroom. Ice Queen, he called her. Watching Ben Casey, enthralled by symptoms, they sat together guessing diagnoses, arguing over diabetes or polio. Being right was a trigger. Their tireless repartee fell drop by drop into a bucket of bleach in hot water. His parents' house key languished in the pocket of his black chinos. Ira spit into his palm. He summoned trumpet, guitar, cornet, nuzzled her neck. She had developed endocrine blockage otherwise referred to as sluggish glands. A riff of tongue played chopsticks along his shoulder, her glossy gold eyelids drooped as they always did after too many dazzling oriflammes. They adopted one calico cat and kept it in a grapefruit carton. Barbara's vocation—mail order—spread across their three rooms, in stacks, avoiding all controversy.

Don't say no, Ira. Just say yes.

As her lips moved, she opened blouse buttons, removed cuff links. Ira dropped a forty-five of *Purple Haze*, humming along like a wasp, pulling her away from the *Post*.

Put down the Epsom salts.

He guided her uncritical fingers, arousing fortune.

He displayed home-made cardboard stencils of gourds, apples, grapes in baskets, vegetables in clusters, flying birds. Also displayed were two silos done with tin in green and brown, their price was higher. Snow had been shoveled along the curb, the newsagent's voice grated while traffic built as did his restlessness. He sensed approaching calamity. An eight-legged spider (frisky, compact), high-stepped up his sticky neck.

An out-of-towner asked, Price?

Stupid hick, the prices are stuck on each silo, also on each theorem. Ira rudely hissed.

Gourds or grapes, dear?

Grapes.

We'll take the grapes.

The word *dear* made hackles rise as the spider entered the ear maw, its best foot forward. The tourist browbeat him to lower the price. Anxious for an end to the workday, he did so he could disassemble his table that folded into a suitcase. Snow flurries festooned the St. Moritz Hotel, caused taxi congestion. Sixth Avenue was covered with wooden boards. He had a hundred and thirty-eight dollars in the money roll.

His whirligigs clanged, whirred in a cold vagrant wind while Ira waited on the shore for the ship to dock—Dover—Calais. His stock included one miniature windmill, one pinwheel, weathervanes made from metal and wood, also one woodsman painted green in two shades with an axe-wielding propeller arm that spun faster as the wind gusted. Also there was a goose with wings (butter-colored) and a cat modeled after Vigilante, Vera's recently acquired tiger cat. The cat's tail flapped when the blade turned. The price per whirligig was twenty pounds. His biggest seller had metal gears that propelled a wooden couple to fornicate. Another good seller – a red weathervane (with orange and green propeller) beside which a black dog wagged a red tail. Ira had on red wool gloves with the fingertips cut away. In the distance the late train from Ramsgate was finally visible around the back of town below the Norman Castle. Another train emerged behind the chalk cliff. Travelers with bundles, umbrellas, bad moods, stamped toward the dock. Two cyclists (a Norwegian, a Swiss), bayed the words "duty free" as Ira hawked. Sun could make a big difference. The schedule gave the times for Brighton, Eastbourne, Bournehouth, Hastings and Folkestone. Jewish percussion wearing leggings and brown-khaki (also wide-brimmed hats) stood together on the staging area. The men carried knapsacks, had water bottles on ropes. The women wore kerchiefs, were clinging, sobbing farewell, shouting, Remember me! above the lilt of the ships' horn. There were chalk markings on their frock coats.

One yelled, *Knackers*!

One queried, Kerosene? Anyone?

Ira had some. He unscrewed the top of the can, looked inside for evaporation, found condensation.

The price?

He shrugged. Whatever you think it's worth.

The voice, a xylophone, questioned, Worth?

Coming or going? Ira asked

Jewish rumblings but no reply to his question.

Thank the boy, someone inserted.

He's not a boy.

Going, came a reply, said with deep feeling by a hairy man.

Ira looked at their secretive faces, saw bleak jaws, G major looks ending in G minor sighs. He needed to wait for the boat to empty before it could fill.

What's your hurry? Who's chasing you?

We'll miss our flight.

The sun's sudden radiance splashed ambience onto their black *yarmulkes* and Ira's balsa stick stuck into his green headband. Why weep? he wondered. Weeping people miss a flight. So sad. Yes, it is sad, he choked. His neck filled up so he sucked a zinc lozenge, rolled up his shirtsleeves, pulled off the cashmere scarf (a gift from Barbara's mother, Evie).

Where to? he asked the group, Dunkerque? Oostende? Zeebruge? Boulogne? Or back to Victoria? Waterloo? Charring Cross?

Someone called out an address in London. He wrote on a scrap of paper: *Stokenchurch Street off New King's Road. Take Fulham Broadway District Line tube. It's cheap. Tell them I sent you, send greetings, remember me – Ira G.* He offered to share the contents of his grease-spotted paper sack containing grilled carrots, green beans and spinach but his offer was refused as though horses' oats had been offered. Cellists strummed at the quayside, a lesser a of G (act of God) he decided, dashing up the ship's ramp, and stopping to look back at the unimmunized immigrants. He saw unappetizing herring lunches spread out on their laps, took in the sight of bronze women hounding quartz men, hungry, long-suffering people wracked with rancor and timidity. Ira felt snubbed, his clarion call ignored. The melted alloy, his face, the venue for their disdain. Not one of ours, their looks had said. Ira continued to watch from the ship's timber railing, saw them spread bread with *shmaltz* (chicken fat) and eat their smelly herrings. He imagined chewing noise like Eli made. The ship set sail. He spit a peppercorn into the wake, making a small dent in the North Sea. Before the sound of the engines became the overpowering noise, he heard a megaphone from the landing site cackle: Ribbons, pins, buttons, duty free. *Bulki* (rolls), hard boiled eggs, plum wine…

A sailor in navy blue wool threaded back and forth, circled the deck as sea birds hung back. He'd left a mint bookmark at page twenty-six of the paperback. Scared to say *Bonjour,* needing more space, he hurried to the café on the upper deck where the mint sprig was lost in the wind. He discovered pralines in the lunch bag. A praline, a good book, a journey. What joy! he thought and read:

He merely asked himself, as a man of the world, 'Does she or does she not, get away with it?' And the answer was in the negative. She was at once too obvious and too obscure. The really incredible thing was that she did not seem to want to get away with it, that she did not seem to understand the urge, the push to get away with it at all costs. He knew, for instance, that she had not a penny of her own. After all that time she had not saved a penny.

He had a postcard to send to Tony showing the Tower of London and wrote *Brahms* but meant bronze. He signed the postcard, *I.* Using the postcard as the new bookmark, he put the book away

and forced himself back to the French lesson. He
had with him *Liberté est un Mot Vietnamien*.

Someone leapfrogged over to his table clutching
Lexique Succinct de l'Érotisme.

The intruder asked, Are you Daniel Cohn-Bendit
or his brother, Jean-Gabriel?

Her lips popped when she added, *Merde*!

She had moist eyelids, moist lips, narrow shoulders, her arm bore welts.

Cohn-Bendit's old. Maybe thirty. Do I look that
old?

Her lips said, *Oui*.

He pined for peanut butter. She was right.

She ordered, *Lémon fraise*.

Her thumbs oscillated between the table rim and
heaven.

Daniel's a vengeful Jew, are you?

He thought, Am I vitriolic? Fainthearted? Grasping? A daddy figure? Mr. Moskowitz on tour? Why
would she think such a thing? but replied, Mrs. Moskowitz went to the doctor, he told her. So what's your
problem, the doctor asked? I can't pee. Hmmm. How
old are you, Mrs. Moskowitz? Eighty-one. Don't you
think you've peed enough?

The girl removed a wire ring from a hole in her
left ear and rubbed the lobe.

So, if I'm a *pisherkeh*, you're a *pisher* too. *Oder gor
oder gornit* (all or nothing), she quipped.

Ira liked her voice. He liked, had always liked, a sympathetic voice that spoke in a language he didn't understand. He didn't flinch.

Delilah, would you say that again into my ear? he asked, warm eyes meeting warm eyes.

She whispered, *Shmohawk? Petseleh?*

✦

Ira carried three passports even when he went to the movies, the taverna, the beach, the toilet, the market, the refrigerator or the sink. For safety he tucked them into the inside pocket of the red leather jacket that he hung on the back of a chair or draped over the knob of the door. He was known in the village as Big Lox, the name Penny had given him. Penny and Ira could live on potato salad, would throw oregano or mountain thyme in with the cooling potatoes. Penny liked to make potato casserole, adding peas and carrots to their terra-cotta dish. Once in a blue moon she made mashed potatoes crowded with a jam of cucumber, onion, garlic and chicory. Penny was the new girl. She bought potatoes by the sack, could cook lamb and macaroni in a single roasting pan (a whole leg) along with a pound of number thirty-nine macaroni, smidgens of oregano, garlic by the handful. They ate three cold lamb lunches three days in a row. Late at night, sitting high up in the fly box, the leftover, now gray, lamb gave off a strong smell.

Deadpan, a deep rut in his forehead, Penny would chide him, Relax, Jewish Julius Caesar. Be frank, please.

His parasites cha-cha'd and fawned in his bowel, clung like stuffed shirts to tetracycline tablets. Something instigated a pain that gripped like iron. Penny's hair was tomato red. She had a map of Brazil on the back of her black Chinese jacket and dried sand had blown into its blowsy wide cuffs. Penny shooed newborn flies and fissioning gnats by waving ring-filled fingers. She caught Ira's eye, winced with a welter of longing. She suggested, A roll in the hay?

If it wasn't mockery in her voice, he was game. He dropped five beefy fingers onto her hair. He swaggered between sincerity and self-consciousness. His legs were rubbery.

Now? he asked.

He moved his hand down to her bony buttocks, fitting it into his palm like a catechism. He heard the word *pasha* as she pushed against him. Up on a dizzying aerie, his desire stepped in quicksand. His shoulders stooped though his tongue tingled. He craved something. He didn't know what so he cut a ringlet of her hair with his fancy Swiss army knife. This old knife had a main blade, a screwdriver, a sewing eye, a scissors, a nail file/cleaner, a bottle opener, a flathead screwdriver, a wire stripper, a lanyard ring and an awl/reamer/tweezers. He regretted that its toothpick had gotten lost in a Berlin restaurant after *K*önigin-*suppe*. He'd had it since Scout days. At night he tossed his all-cotton black turtleneck XL/46-48 across the knife. Its sleeves were frayed, had turned dull from washing. At night he dropped his keys on top of the knife and turtleneck, all except the one key that he'd swallowed in lovemaking. As the room refilled with flies, Penny kneeled down. She pressed his fingertips to her lips. She breathed in, pressed her cheek against the back of his hand. Her head shook when his tongue shot out to lick her hair.

Ira and Papusca (doll) walked toward the fisherman's house. It was newly whitewashed, like confectioners' sugar. Papusca inserted her thumb into his mouth. He tasted a vegetable stock.

Are you hungry? he asked, thinking of amber chicken broth with noodles and boiled chicken that would fall apart in his mouth.

Suck it?

He didn't want to. He would want to without being asked but, once asked, he resisted. His resistance was hard as an olive, also salty, withered, briny, resinous and gummy. The word yes got caught in his throat. He's weary, thought Papusca, examining his day-old stubble at a derisory slant while Ira brooded, gazed out the window. He was soaked in ardor but uneasy. He saw two figures walking between the cypresses, luminous in the midday sun. They were feathered and plumed and the cypresses were bleeding. His resistance evaporated. He licked her broth-coated thumb until the brine was gone, shut then opened his eyes. A brown earthworm dropped from a bird's beak onto his shoulder. Papusca stood up, brushed his lips with hers. Dreamily, he shuffled his deck of cards, dealt a fan of six overlapping cards. Like Ma, he thought, all the indices are visible. He fanned six cards six times under his arm and snatched egg slices one by one, dipping each into wine, adding coarse salt. He smoothed her cashmere-like hair. When he bit a cracker, tears filled his eyes and nose. He blinked, blinked. The bird dove down and roosted above him on the orange tiles where rye bread was stacked up (half a loaf) beside the bowl of tangerines (whose dry green leaves were still attached but crumbling off) that had turned to gray mold. Their water carrier (a pail on each shoulder) had left his motor running, sending vibrations through the house. He deposited two pails of water at their door. Ira felt Papusca's hand under his collar, while her fingers slid across the shoulder blade. He unbuttoned her dress, took a swallow of ginger ale. Her hand closed over a honey-colored beeswax candle that was so malleable it curled as she clasped it. A shutter banged. All the shutters banged.

She was seventeen. Her name was Sylvia. She was a genie, released from sexual objectification, two years with an old ram as his dishrag. After swimming against ferocious ocean cross-currents she took a short cut through the peach orchard and drank a can of condensed milk as soon as she walked through the door. Pale rose wallpaper with butter-flies, chimpanzees and pianos hung askew from all the walls. To please her, Ira wore her gift – leather underpants. He was hairy above and below. She carried two black plastic bags, was still wrapped with a towel. She turned a bag upside down. Out spilled hard-on drops (coconut-flavored) and Spanish fly drops (strawberry-flavored from historic Mexico). From the other bag tumbled Rough Rider studded condoms. For herself: a transparent red nylon French maid outfit with white lace trim. For both: soap, orgy oil, erection crème, Anal Eze, extend, quirt, English handcuffs. Sylvia used overpowering verbs when she spoke, had spots like measles on her shoulder blades, was futureless, without money. She had cloudy gray eyes, hardy lips, an abundance of freckles on her nose, was moodless and dragged around a dangerous Jack Russell terrier.

While she brewed strong coffee Ira emptied a paper bag. Out poured onion and sesame bagels. They sat together. Sylvia chewed gum and half a bagel with feta at once. To keep her from getting a chill, Ira wrapped his towel around her hair. When he finished eating his bagel, he ate another while eyeing her half-eaten bagel. The sunlight glinted across the oilcloth table in a *fleur-de-lis* pattern while the sea bashed against the pilings under the house. In one bite, he wolfed down her leftover.

Coffee, please.

He dipped his fist inside her panties, felt muscled terra firma and rolled it around the hairy database. As always, she spiraled and his compass needle quivered. He pulled off her panties and sank onto his boxy, achy knees, pressing her fresh onion roll against his face.

The jittery, cinnamon-colored hound whined and scraped its nails against the floor. Sylvia's ermine-textured hair dangled. He tried to shoo the dog, got silent, bit his lip when he heard Sylvia wail and felt fists pulling hunks of head hair. Her knobby legs parted while he held fast to the back of her daffodil thighs. It was more than an hour before a shower of wanderlust doused him. When it did, thoughts and more thoughts paraded by: It's time to leave this place or she'll cannibalize me like soft cheese. What about the money tree? Am I cretinized by bagel eating? Am I a victim of self-derision? If only someone had given me a dime for milk every morning and I'd saved the dimes, I could have had a sling-shot, and my money tree wouldn't have been bare.

Get that look off your face, Sylvia injected, squatting down to catch her breath.

Her eyes turned bright orange while her hands revolved and coiled into fists. She wasn't balanced in her crouch pose, so she took off and flew past him and landed on the windowsill. Her next utterance was inaudible when the hard spikes of her tail made a majestic pounding sound. By then he was excited again but the leather was constraining. Lunch would wait. He scattered her bag of toys across the bagel crumbs/onion scraps/poppy seeds and the oozing Camembert in order to reach for the French maid outfit in high humor. From the corner of his eye he watched as she deposited a clump of fresh, glistening eggs on the sill. Saucy also, she flew against his back and gripped him from behind. From there she unzipped him, looping around his back and festooning his dangler with a Rough Rider condom.

✦

Ira was restless. The knot returned. Lonely middle age. When Barbara visited, she suctioned him. All the while his *kepi* raced, plans were small chains with interlinking links. With little retention, the links broke open, DNA spilled out in arabesques. When Barbara displayed no interest in his kisses or in repatriation, the knot tightened. Barbara impressed everyone in the village in exactly the same way − as faithful. She had a bad ear, was ungainly, often shy. She had large feet, wore a watch. She moved with no speed, was aglow (as in saintly) with astral eyes. Her mind was uncluttered. She'd saved enough money for the house and paid for it in cash. They swore to each other they'd settle down. Wrapping a Matisse beach towel around his shoulders, Barbara snipped hair hanging over Ira's ears. Barbara's cheeks showed a dash of high color, her mink voice rewarded submission with submission. She asked him for a Limoges china cup for her birthday, had given him mint-colored mittens for his. Leave here! Go out for eggs, don't come back. Tell her I must go to my parents' house. My parents are ill. They need me. May need me. Those same … Leave her? What would I do with my things if I go? What things are important? The reels in cans are. How to carry them away? Where to store them? I'm ill at ease with heavy loads, with packing, also storage. Of course, she might leave first.

With a limp voice, Barbara simpered, I need seed money.

Ira misunderstood. She had meant for the grove and the beds. He thought she meant for the radiating étoile that was protected by a scarecrow. As usual in collision, her eyes followed the flight of his oscillating, repeating thoughts.

Can't you read my mind? Good. Read it.

Gray strands of hair crossed his skull. Once his hair was only flecked with gray, but that was no more. All references Barbara made to gray hair were platitudes. Outside: A field. A tractor. A new motorway. A band of gypsies were their closest neighbor and lived in a freshly painted blue castle without doors or window frames. They'd strung the turret on the castle with tiny Christmas lights. Ira counted. I've lived in her goddamned houses counting this one for thirty-five seasons. Everything I own is packed into one closet. My reels in cans are under the couch, chafing the caramel fabric. I came for lunch on February 6th. Our overnight is as old as the toffee tomcat is. She owns it all. I own nothing. The toffee tomcat had a talented rolling tongue, ate azure blue and murre eggs with blood-red yolks and would dive like a swan onto Barbara's empty lap.

One gray day Barbara asked Ira, Would you mind a tiered cake?

How many tiers?

Three ... four?

Have five, he grandly agreed.

Royal icing?

Sure.

Yellow marzipan?

Natch.

When the tomcat leapt, the discussion dropped.

Ira suggested, Let's start over?

Barbara listened while he emptied trash baskets. In them: shavings, avocado skins, cigarette ash and butts. When tying plastic handles in knots, a broken smile crossed his lips. Dumping garbage (his exercise) brought instant gratification. Scanning the room, he saw no new prospects for filling more bags. Monkeylike, the cat climbed up Barbara's sweater. The flow of oxygenated blood (not energized but heavy) played tag with his cerebral process. He considered sex his sixth sense. If not for sex and food, why live? He prepared a large clam for lunch by breaking the shell with a hammer. Inside a fleshy, gray mound. He cut it into pieces. At the counter, Barbara prepared celery hearts (minced). She splat in ketchup, green onion (minced), lemon juice, horseradish (creamed), hot pepper sauce (three dashes). Ira added a dash of HP Sauce. Also Worcestershire – large dash, small dash.

Postpone your appointment? she begged, meaning his boxing lesson. Talk to me about something.

He sat in his chair at the table and was about to dredge up a joke when she asked, Don't you plan to shave? Are you going to sit there in your underwear all day?

He stood up. In the mirror he saw an anemic face. He *did* need a shave, saw a randy goat looking back. A deck of unwelcome thoughts fanned out: My ring is stuck. Why not shrimp too? Why no crystal glasses filled with iced white? Why no ice cream with nuts and cicadas or cheese with holes? He scooped up a slice of clam, dipped it in sauce. Ate another. Barbara chewed slowly. Still hungry, he eyed what remained on the plate.

Have them if you like. Have them all, she offered and pushed the plate toward him.

With one stab of his fork he speared everything and picked up the plate in order to drink the sauce like melted ice cream.

Ira read as though walking along a beach looking for shells. His eyes skimmed whole sentences, para-

graphs, moved diagonally down entire pages. He retained nothing. Barbara bought herself an eggplant
chiffon dress. Hourly thrusts of old, now monthly –
twenty or thirty minutes of golden lather followed by
sinking dismay.

We wait so long … Let's not wait.

You're so right.

I know.

He tied a dishtowel around his waist, stood at the
sink scrubbing and rinsing a bucketful of fresh clams,
chopping up shallots. She loves me. Chops onions.
She loves me not. Minces garlic. She needs me.
Grinds white pepper. She needs me not. Chops basil
from her garden, also coriander leaves. She desires
me? Throws in leftover rice from the saucepan and
washes the pan. She lusts not? He melts butter with
pepper flakes and white pepper, stirs in an egg yolk,
adds heavy cream, also milk. She'll take care of me
if I get sick? He tosses in a half bottle of dry white
wine. She'll leave if I get sick? He adds the small
clams to the pot. If she goes back, I will too.

Lower the heat, she called out. Snooker! Lower
the heat!

The fire went out. He lit it again and sat on the
floor at her feet, laying his head on her lap waiting
for their food. He fit his palm across her cheek, could
almost fit her whole face in one hunky hand, but the
tide had come in. Barbara dipped her hands into
leftover melted butter laced with pepper. She dusted

his nose with butter and pepper causing him to reach around and grip her peach-shaped shoulders.

Powdered snow, then wet snow, fell. Droplets of ice coated the windows. The temperature in Brooklyn, five degrees. Barbara grated sharp cheddar against the rusted aluminum grater, mashed in pimiento and mayonnaise and spread swatches of the mix across rye bread. Snow covered the dead cherry tree on the (also dead) lawn. Under her arm he saw ginger-colored sprouts and turned her in her tracks. A butter knife with pimiento smear froze mid-slice, clutched in her fist. He lifted her arm to expose the endearing bristle to electric light, leaned into the shell-shaped armpit, kissed and smelled evocative musk. Tears came to his eyes. She softened too. Mixed in, he'd seen a smattering of white hairs that were not there last week, not there two months before when he'd looked closely while in the shower.

So, when? What now?

✦

Into the wind flew rubbish, relics, shards. He carried nine x-rays. The x-rays (twenty-seven remaining teeth) demystified fillings, bridges, caps, gum surgeries, broken bonding, chips where he used them to open beer bottles. One tooth hung by two roots. Omelet bits were caught in gaps. He used the corner of the manila envelope to extricate omelet and to scratch the rash spreading across his lower back. Scratching provoked spaghetti coils and irrefutable relief. Nothing hurt until the dentist (yawning between jabs made by a calibrated probe into the gum pockets) finished the consultation and presented him with an estimate for twelve thousand dollars. Dr. Tusk (who had three sons at Columbia University) outlined a plan. First phase: Dental visits, oral hygiene, cultures, scaling, root planing, extraction of number two (the hanging tooth), re-evaluation after that. Second phase: Bone graft, implants, more extractions, replace old fillings, a night guard to stop the grinding. His tongue, a daubing handkerchief, tapped the achy places. There was a wire protruding from the old bridge that cut his tongue.

A difficult patch, he told Tusk. Can you lop them all? Sure.

Three strands of thought: What would this cost in Juarez? I can't get all the debris out of the crevices anymore. I do recant every flossless night.

I mean to floss, Dr. Tusk. I don't know if I grind at night. Oh, what would titanium implants cost?

Sixty thousand dollars.

I wasn't aware of an abscess until you poked into my gum with that metal probe.

Passing an ants' nest in a blossoming pear tree, the white blossoms reminded him of fresh popcorn. Ira pushed through the swinging door wishing for sweet Veracruz oysters. He patted the ticket in his jacket. After the session at the blood bank (the painless pinprick, orange juice carton, atoms of oxygen), he clutched his portfolio made from chamois-like leather (a gift from Minx) under his arm. Minx was the Chinese acupuncturist's receptionist/assistant. He pined for Minx and for Jericho, Minx' progeny, and worried about rheumatic aches in his knees that might just be fluid retained from too much salt. Before Minx would treat his fizzing joint pain with clotted yogurt, her hand churned an old goatskin. While she worked, Ira pressed his knees together with neck bowed, hoping the sun would appear and heat his joints. He sat all morning on the chocolate-brown Mies van der Rohe chair ruminating on why Minx got so elated by success with clotted yogurt. When elated, her hormones squirted against her white robe. Her hands milked his knee of pain. He watched the clock. Tangled wild roses, lilies, unraveling tulips clung together in a water glass on a china plate engulfed with eggs and chips.

Carping and eating, what else do we need, dollie?

I need you to speak Dutch or German or French or Russian to me.

She laughed and (before the sun set), quoted bits of poems in three of the four languages he'd mentioned.

Ira dropped his peaked cap onto the bed, tossed the portfolio away while fending off Jericho, whose tongue was dripping and slobbering gravel bits in an affectionate exhibition. As Ira tweaked Jericho on the nose, Jericho's red eyes blinked squeamishly. Honey bees buzzed and zoomed. The watch Ira wore told precise time, fatalistic to the minute. He batted Jericho back, good-natured. In white veil, holding white blossoms, the cool breeze lifted her hair. Minx had wine on ice, the best mousetrap, a leg-up, was studying engineering. Her specialty: electromagnetic theory, gravitational mass, velocities. The window filled with light. Crab apples dangled, casting dark shadows to and fro against the wood frame cottage. Ira's hands were deep in the pockets of his overcoat, a drop in the bucket, a viola and cello duet stirred the air. It couldn't be dementia. He couldn't be a stuffed shirt. The canker on his nostril made him queasy, the week-long growth of facial hair wasn't Rabelaisian in the slightest. Their chimney had become clogged by a bird's nests and neither he nor Minx could find the gas meter. Nonetheless, she plowed his furrow and he hers after which they shared a drop of sherry. For run-on seasons he squatted like Jonah inside the whale, played musical chairs between encounters, ate from a bucket of unwashed apples. Chewing in melody, Jericho (the interloper), barged into the dingy chrome room. Ira regretted eating five pieces of (Eli's favorite) Almond Roca Buttercrunch because (like a time bomb) it activated the esophagitis (pain), another ever-expanding ticking clock. To make matters worse, he could no longer control gas, fury, guilt, heartburn, crux, halo, fork in the road.

Vera hollered during the telephone call, You've outlived Tony. Tony is dead at age forty-seven in Halle. He died ten steps from the church of St. Moritz, collapsed carrying Harriet's …

Who is Harriet?

His wife.

How do you know?

Melba sends us a Christmas card every year. Melba told me Harriet ran to the bronze statue of Handel, froze, ran on to Roland, froze… But, in the square, she found a priest who caught on, dashed with Harriet to the mismatched vinyl suitcases …

That's right, make fun of a dead boy's luggage.

… Tony, a rag. The priest asked Harriet, Are you Catholic? She told him, Very. He choked. You'll never meet her. You'll never see his children – Patricia or Michael Ira. Michael Ira Mogliani. Did you hear what I said?

Ira reviewed his last meeting with Tony at John's on Bleecker Street eating pizza after the funeral of Mr. S., their Scout leader. While Tony wiped Ira's spire with a clean handkerchief, removed ghastly surgical tape, they drank two pitchers of beer in glass mugs. The subjects they discussed: Twelve pounds lost. Raw fruits. Raw vegetables. Fishing. Tony's eyes were peacock feathers, his tic woke between bites of cheese and mushroom pizza. He had on a hanging lavaliere. When had he begun to resemble his mother down to arm patting with earth-colored fingers and a warm rumble in his voice? While Ira shot the shit, Tony shook cayenne onto the hot cheese, and, when Tony spoke, Ira sprinkled Parmesan on top of that. Their lives were not parallel but both were self-justified and self-taught. Also: No hospitals, no brothels, no jails, not authoritative, no gimmicks, not factual, maudlin, spice-eaters, had cold feet. After pizza they'd walked on the gravel path, discussed alcids with beaks holding fish. Tony explained how to reach him. Ira took out his pen, used a locksmith's receipt as a scrap. Fugitive Boulevard, Tony told him. Ira wrote *Futch … Futurt … Fu …* went blank. The word was unspellable. He covered the receipt with his palm. Number? He asked. He wrote *14*. Ira asked the name of the town, faked the rest *14 Flick … flik?… tale … tail?*

Tony held Ira's hand with two fingers. A film covered his eyes while he stared into the mustard face of his watch. Tony invited, You'll come and see me if I get married? Meet my wife and teach my kids to fish? Ira squeezed back, told him, For sure. We'll take them for a bike ride!

The first white nostril hair sprouted. The score was rising. White on head, in eyebrows, armpits, pubis, finally in his nose. Ira spit at the bushfire, gazed into the distance in beatific preoccupation, a handful of analgesic capsules in the pocket of his leather jacket. Also in that pocket, echinacea taken with food and yohimbe taken with Minx, while looking into her taffy-colored eyes. The waters of Galilee lapped continually as nets dried against black basalt in white heat. Eyeless and wingless insects nested in droves. Here the heat was different from other heats, it burned like fire, so his shirt was wide open, his skin sticky, an invitation to insects. As he stepped across a trench, he saw not even a trickle of water or milk. The old walled city was burnished with sunlight. Roving mules, stooped from great weight, carried limestone away from the quarry toward unfertile fields. Ira's dim white hands fisted, the knuckles soothed by the oven-like heat though his joints felt hollow. He pulled off a vine that brushed his head, tossed it onto the ground, tried to crush it with his leather boot but the annoying vine got tangled up until he shook it into a ravine below the *dunam* of stone Crusader markings. Lamb and camel turds made a monotonous boundary along asphodels, beside amber boulders. A large cat with a spotted coat hunted for hare.

Further along, stood young Aleppo pines in rows, their roots exposed breaking through mosaic pavement fragments. Ira sat on a stone, unwrapped folded waxed paper. He bit into olive and sliced mutton on thick bread, played at rolling an orange around with the toe of his boot. A drop of Minx's birch oil dressing squeezed out from between the bread as he bit down. Crumpling the waxed paper, he thought again, smoothed it, tore a strip, folded a smart edge and slid it between his teeth, pushing mutton gristle, bitter dark ash and pasty dun-colored gluten out. Thirsty, he tapped a cone, collected sweet palm sap to wet his whistle. I'll take a bath, he decided, Sink, let my arms float. He whiffed urine, wondered what animal had marked the place on which he sat. Justifiably comfortable, porridge thoughts lumping up, connecting dots, his belly was filled. Mutant worms (cylindrical, one millimeter long, self-mating, with nine-day life spans), had infested his bowel. Ira ran a fever, wore two sweaters for warmth. He wrapped a scarf with moon and guitar designs in olive and black around his neck.

He's wretched, he heard Minx tell Jericho, heard Jericho beat wings against the door, hurling clots.

Minx brought him onion and garlic tea.

You must drink it down scalding hot, Petsky.

Jericho lurked at the door covering his peepee. His feet were wide apart as he glared at Ira's salt-and-pepper stubble. Minx admitted that Ira was nothing like Lenin, more like Napoleon with black boots beside the bed, nose and eyes outlined with sweat shine, eye rims vermilion.

His plumbing wasn't right. Have I crossed into diabetes? Overeaten? Turned into an ape? He was wary of the onion-laced garlic tea because his teeth couldn't take heat. He turned a cold eye on Jericho. What to eat without onions? If I need a hospital, then what? He had no experience with hospitals or institutions. What four-legged beast would nuzzle his neck if he left? No longer talky, not fun, he ate horrible food, except crisp bacon when Minx was away, spent death row nights with an axe, a quiver and mace at his bedside. A non-individual with unresolved sexual appetite, he never finished eating. He fell asleep but immediately woke because something was missing – its second letter was an "o," last letter an "a." More *himself* after sleep (nine, ten, eleven hours) Ira regressed, got prayerful. Burning and shivering, he pulled the wool blanket up to his neck, stuck his hands between his thighs while Minx piled another wool blanket (her striped cream and salmon Hudson Bay) over him.

Now. Sweat it out, Petsky.

He heard flutes, oboes in E-flat, clarinet, bassoon, horn, trumpet, trombone, a tuba, timpani, harp, piano, also jousting strings like cherry petals falling. The music brought Vera's tirade on Stravinsky to mind. Vera abhorred Stravinsky, would snap: Debussy's pastel washes! Your Stravinsky is green, ghastly. And Eli would swear by Stravinsky, a guaranteed tirade on dissonance. Blah blah blah. Ira wondered, Did they change their phone number? Then Vera phoned him, shouted, Come for Easter? Stay for Passover?

Minx brought the mail to his bed, also the *Herald Tribune.* Ira unwrapped his package. Inside, a tin of Almond Roca Buttercrunch and an airmail envelope stuffed with photographs of whippets, a tiger cat and a newspaper clipping from *Art News,* the Exhibitions section highlighted in yellow. He read:

The artist will attend if health allows

His mood skewed. Had Eli been recognized? Anxious about the clipping, so many stark white hairs, needing iodine for the cat's claw cut along his palm, he swung his legs over the side of the high bed, sprang onto the flokati and sank into the aluminum and nickel tubular chair. Was that man still daubing grist on canvas? Was he stopping the clock? Wasn't he unabashed by failure? *Why* hadn't his bravado waned along with his virility? Ira scratched the rash. The years were hazy. How long had Vera had whippets not dachshunds? How old was this cat? He was certain there had been no white hair on his body when he last sat over fried egg and ketchup sandwiches with Eli and Vera at a Greek coffee shop while they waited for his train. Three years ago? Six years ago? Was it ten years ago?

LONG DAY'S JOURNEY INTO DAY

At the stile, the official eyed Ira with perplexity. The official asked, Passport?

An old, lonely boy, Ira had no ass left, wore a short red leather jacket over a once black turtleneck jersey, tight jeans, showing his age when he called them dungarees. He lowered his eyelids while trolling through the blue and white plastic KLM bag, fluttering fine brown lashes. He handed the official a passport.

The official examined it, pushed it back, demanded, Passport?

Ira fished again. He knew them by feel, reinserted the sienna one, bypassed the Venetian-red and pulled out the dog-eared mars-brown-colored passport. The official passed the scanner across it. When the computer screen registered he was waved across the border. Between the stile and pyramid Ira stepped through a door labeled with a human stick figure logo. Next to it, the stick figure of a bird, an X through its wings. Crossing into the room, he stood before the porcelain urn. Wary of the elevator, he took the stairway. When he reached the pyramid he was still shaky but the suitcase was waiting. He looked around with fearsome eyes, was unsure as to which direction to go, so he sat down on a long narrow bench. He entirely cleared his throat of phlegm that had gathered in the fifteen or so hours of travel. As he had come from east to west it was not very much later in the day than when he began the journey. He'd awakened at dawn, had coffee, gone to the airport, had breakfast, gotten on the aircraft, had breakfast, changed planes, had Italian coffee, boarded a larger airplane, been given breakfast, drinks, a large lunch. Now, it was not quite noon – a long day's journey into day. Of course it was the same day and still lunchtime.

He looked up at the illuminated board covered with symbols and arrows: There was a cigarette crossed with an X and an onion crossed with an arrow. The letters WC below an arrow pointing towards the door he'd just closed. Also: An automobile logo. A bus logo. £¥€$. A snail with an X through its shell. A cup with a rising, neon lightning rod bisected by an arrow surrounded by a neon ring. He spit what he'd gathered from his esophagus into a tissue and followed the cup logo arrow. In the coffee bar he asked for a double Ivory Coast with coronet of chicory. He drank it and his heart rang like a telephone bringing good news. He had another double and buckled a jeweled dagger onto his belt. He was ready to offer his services to his old/estranged/dying parents.

Wait! Shechina told him, and shut the door in his face.

He pressed the button on his stopwatch and let it go until Shechina (wearing a hairnet) opened the door once more. Six minutes and thirty-two seconds had passed.

No visitors, she explained.

But I'm the son!

Come back later … for lunch.

She looked him over coldly, wasn't swayed though he beseeched her with his affecting face. It took him ten minutes to walk back down the hill past the shallot and scallion field, past the war cemetery to the white sandy beach marked by painted oil drums. He ate lunch at a coffee shop. He seethed. A violet-colored rash, like a belt, developed around his waist. When he left the mosquito-infested restaurant by way of a hallway, he walked back along the sandy beach and, instead of passing the war cemetery again, climbed across the dry riverbed over which a slow train was crossing on a trestle. His boots were soaked with the aroma of scallions pleasantly mixed with the scents from the hillside lemon groves. It was necessary to walk the long way around thick shrubbery.

Once again he confronted the dilapidated house. This time he didn't ring the bell but reached into his pocket, retrieved a handful of detritus that included nail clippings (not his own), one black and white die, cherry pits, crushed banknotes, key, coins, toothpicks, dental floss. He withdrew the key, blew off crumbs mixed into bits of flug and fitted it into the lock. The door swung on its old hinges. Ira emptied the pits and clippings onto the ground, returned what remained, including the key, to his pocket and wiped his palm across his hip. He stepped inside and dropped the KLM bag and the suitcase onto a tiger skin just as Vera's jet-black whippets flew at him. He feared these Johnny-come-latelies and brushed them aside. Crossing the living room, he passed his father's studio, his mother's office, his childhood room, the aviary, bypassed the kitchen and Shechina's room, and burst into his parents' dark, west-facing bedroom.

The shades were drawn and it smelled of cooked lamb. He raised the shades. There they were, head to foot on their narrow four-poster, motionless, two sunken-cheeked corpses. Vera was turned on her side. Eli's yellow beard was a meter long and hung limply off the side of the bed. They seemed to have shrunk. Ira thought he might faint. He could swear they were dead and ran to the aviary, pulled a feather out of the tail of Vera's white cockatiel (named Debit) dashed back into the bedroom. He put the feather under Vera's nostrils, saw no movement. The same with Eli. A great nutcracker gripped his chest and squeezed. I've come too late? The pain hopped onto a pogo stick. He gasped, fell onto both knees and doubled over.

Ira's next awareness was of lying fully clothed on the lower bunk bed he'd slept in as a boy. Eli was backlit, hanging onto the door frame.

Eli whispered, Have you had lunch? Have you eaten? Mama's trying to murder me.

Eli's head shook uncontrollably, his voice was in a high register as if sugared. Mama's guillotined my testicles... she fed me opium while I was in a hot bath. It was so hot I didn't feel a thing but when I looked for them later they were gone.

Eli fumbled with his dressing gown but was too feeble to hold onto the doorjamb and pull back the fabric at the same time to reveal the injury, so he shimmied instead. Remembering that he'd come to care for Eli and Vera, Ira lowered his boots onto the floor. His armpit and shoulder pinched terribly.

Let me bring you coffee, Pa. Soup? Eggs? You need fluids!

Eli looked as if he would collapse. His quivering beard reached his knees. Eli gasped, Bring goose liver. Please. Onion soup. Peppermint liqueur. That's all I can digest.

In spite of the pain, Ira went to find Shechina but she had gone to the market and the kitchen was in turmoil. He filled the kettle that was burnt black and gray-khaki with grease and searched for a match. He checked under plates piled with fish bones but found no matches. On the table was a dark chocolate cake with cat prints across the icing missing one slice. There were brown chocolate animal prints along the floor. He opened all the cabinets but couldn't find a match, bent to look underneath the sink, saw wine bottles, checked the sugar bowl, found banknotes. The rash girding his middle itched. He grabbed a fork in order to scratch under the jersey. The rash was spreading, a puddle was seeping from the kettle.

Never fill it to the top, it leaks.

It was his mother's voice. He turned and saw her. She was shrunken, her skin now mottled, eyes glazed. She gripped the refrigerator door.

Stand aside, she hollered. I'll fix it!

Her voice rattled. Her hands were transparent with brown spots, nonetheless they moved quickly. She struck a match. From where it came, Ira couldn't tell. She lit the fire, tossed away half the water in the kettle.

Don't scratch that, you've drawn blood. When was the last time you had your teeth looked at? Don't you brush them? You obviously didn't use the money I sent to fix them …

She separated the gall bladder from the goose liver, salted water in a bowl, soaked the liver in it, removed it with a fork and set it on a wrought iron skillet, sprinkling paprika, sugar and ginger, adding goose fat and began to sauté.

Sit down, Ira. You don't look well.

Ma, Pa told me that you've sliced off his balls. Is he losing his mind?

No such thing. I performed a merciful orchiectomy. He didn't feel a thing I assure you since his bath water would have scalded anyone but him, and then added, His thick skin!

She glared at her son. Are you afraid I've castrated Papa?

Ira thought: What an idea!

She lowered her voice and spoke as she would to a four-year-old: He doesn't need those testicles anymore.

The goose fat sizzled, setting a delicious odor free.

What do you know? We haven't seen you in seventeen years, two months, twelve days, fourteen hours. But who's counting?

She put three leaded crystal glasses onto a tray and filled each halfway with peppermint liqueur. The sight of the glasses and the smell filling the room made Ira want to cry.

Ira sat at the edge of their bed while they shared the meal. Was she right, had seventeen years passed? He had nothing to show for so many years. No extraordinary memories, no children, no wife, no property, no stock. All he had was a few flopping fish, several well-fed hummingbirds, tender keepsakes in metal cans, reminders of various women; also three passports with official stamps and ink. Had anything ever tasted as good as this goose liver?

Ma, Pa, I'm here to care for you. You're both fail...

Speak for yourself, Eli snapped before Ira could finish the sentence.

Ira watched, astonished, as Eli lit a match and held it under the satin (nylon?) sleeve of Vera's dressing gown that was edged (as was the collar) with Persian lamb. There was a flash of green light. The fabric wrinkled into flame. Vera rolled her flaming self up in the food-stained eiderdown like Cleopatra while Eli grabbed his cane and hit the roll of cotton-covered goose down with a thwack. He lowered his arm, stuck his fist into an olive jar, grabbing his lower plate of teeth and jammed it into his mouth.

Pass the liver, son.

Ira craved more goose liver. Eyeing what was left, he inched the serving plate toward his thigh, then up into his lap away from his father's grasping hand.

That's right, I've come to care for you, Pa.

Ira chewed while softly rubbing the eiderdown in which his mother was rolled. He pulling the corner away, the flame was out. A spool of stiff, brick-red hair sprang out at him. He smelled cooked lamb again, saw that the playing cards from Vera's patience were falling from her night table like autumn leaves. They were two tumbling fours, a falling two of hearts. As the angel Gabriel blew his bannered trumpet, Ira put the palm of his hand on Vera's back, reached his other hand out and touched Eli on the thigh and stroked them both.

Sixty-five years with the same sunflower. Eli wheezed.

Gabriel blew the trumpet again. This blast was inviting, consequential.

Quickly! Get a doctor! Eli begged, Don't separate us. Bury us together.

Eli's jiggles accelerated to the point of tremors.

Take the lantern. Get the doctor.

Ira was blank. Can't Shechina … ?

Eli instructed him, Take the painting on the north wall, it's a map to the next village. The doctor is named Oxn.

There were four paintings on the north wall, all entirely different maps. They were titled: *Priests. Eateries. Truck traffic. Oxn*. Ira snatched that one off the wall.

The route led along a narrow path above the house until it branched off, passing the dump, the Carmelite monastery, crusader buildings, catacombs with stone doors. When two roads met, he bit his lip in confusion. Seeing fig trees, grape vines, pomegranate trees he hurried on. Half a kilometer further stood derelict cars, TV antennas, then a swinging brass shingle.

DOCTOR OXN
MEDICINE AND PHARMACY SINCE 1945

Ira shouted into the intercom, Help!

Behind him crouched dry stark unyielding mountains, beside him, olive trees that had laurel bushes at their bases. The wind blew. A bronze bell rang. Seeing men wielding yellow clubs leaping from buses and trucks, Ira hid behind a large marble column. He filled his pockets with small stones to protect his loins. He looked left, then right, was noticed by a stray dog with its tail chopped away. At a distance what could be a doctor clambered down three front steps, was buttoning a cashmere topcoat, hurrying into a polished black Peugeot. The untethered cashmere scarf caught in the car door when he slammed it shut and was left dragging outside as the engine purred. The car raced away. Ira tried to flag the car. When this failed, he tried to flag another car, but the dog held him at bay. The club-wielding men galloped to and fro shouting insults and slurs. Which is more of a menace, he wondered, the dog, the men, the clubs, ill-fitting boots, coming home, combing thinning hair? He lay on his back beside the column, fought off an urge to masturbate to calm himself in case the dog masturbated too. Looking up at the sky, he watched a lazy cloud cross the sun. His jacket was red, the sidewalk was sienna, the doctor's house was olive green. A flock of turkeys cut a swathe across the road intimidating the dog, antagonizing the club-wielders when a sudden downpour sent turkeys as well as club-wielders running. Water poured, made mud rivulets. Ira stood up so as not to muddy the (too tight) cowboy boots. He could smell his own perspiration and his ribs hurt. Turning the painting around, he retraced his route, noticed TV antennas, Biblical pomegranate trees that were wet with fresh rainwater.

After covering Vera's wrist and elbow in gauze that oozed bright orange jell, Dr. Oxn felt along her right arm in search of enough fat into which he could inject morphine. He touched stretched strings of tough old muscle, realized her eyes were rolling back in her skull made of sugar.

May I brush her hair? pleaded Eli.

Eli picked up her melting brush but got distracted and brushed his own long beard with it. The effort so tired him, he crumpled beside Vera on their four-poster.

He begged, Rouge her cheeks, brush and style her hair.

He was trembling.

Who will read to me while I paint? Feebly, Eli rasped, Give here, and pointed at Vera's pocketbook.

While gauzing the burnt length of neck with one hand, Oxn hoisted up the green leather Hermes bag being pointed out with the other and dropped it onto Eli's chest with a jolt that took Eli's breath away. Eli closed his eyes, the sockets were sunken. Shallow wheezing made Dr. Oxn roll one eye onto Eli's face for a look. This was the fifth visit in two months. Had he brought enough morphine for both? Their cat darted onto the bed, hunkered down, bookmarked by the barely observable outlines of their two skinny asses. It curled into a tiger ball, was named Vigilante by Eli, their third cat with that name. Eli strained to undo the bag's clasp, reached in. He felt for the money roll bound with rubber bands, grasped the wad in his fist and shut his eyes, his hand frozen around the roll. Oxn didn't want to be distracted by the old man. He could find nowhere on Vera to inject morphine except the sole of her foot, and did so. But, afraid not to, he punctured Eli's dropped protuberance, once a buttock, with a second injection of morphine. He wrote a list of instructions for the maid on the back of a blank prescription. When the doctor had gone, Vera's two whippets crept back in and folded themselves into ebony crescents. That area of the eiderdown was smeared with drool, clay, food droppings, paint. These dogs were her sentries during sleep, eating, geriatric lovemaking and now they inched their paws and snouts nearby the frail dying waxed flesh of their beloved fig trees.

✦

Shechina navigated through the market clasping handfuls of beets that had limp greens attached, also spinach, lemons by the sack, small oranges. Dark green dry leaves were attached to these branches along with fragrant swills. Twice Shechina turned to admire a cage of darting, trilling finches hooked to the ceiling of the bread shop while she waited for the fresh bread to make its debut from the stone oven. Claus, the baker, and his son, Clause, the baker, and his son, Clause, never showed her a glimmer of recognition even though she'd shopped at their bakery for years. While dismissing her, the Claus's minced and danced in reverence to customers with good watches. Shechina kept her eyes on the floor. Her short arms hung at her side. When the bakers went to check the oven, she watched the finches. The round loaves (smell first) entered on trays and were thrown into a bin. A big wheel of village bread cost three coins. She paid with lowered eyes, head at right angles to her neck. Walking along the road, she pinched dough out of the fresh bread. By the time she let herself back into the kitchen, the bread was all crust.

Doctor Oxn saw Ira at the intersection where two roads met, stopped his Peugeot and rolled down the window.

Ira asked, So? as a herd of goats reached the intersection.

Some goats went left, some right, stragglers leapt through vines, grazing Ira wickedly.

So?

Sew buttons. the doctor snickered in reply.

Ira got that the doctor had made a joke. It irritated him since he only laughed at his own jokes.

So? Ira asked again, ignoring the joke.

The doctor shook his head.

I've made them comfortable. As comfortable as possible. It's probably a matter of hours or days.

But, she was up making goose liver pate not one hour ago…

I doubt it.

She was. I ate some.

Regardless, they can't last. Arrangements should be made. What are you, son? What are they? What are their wishes?

Ira flushed. I don't know.

The doctor cracked his knuckles. Of course you do. I'll help you make arrangements.

They've never said.

Find out! the doctor counseled, Otherwise we won't know in which cemetery to bury them … if at all.

Goats kept coming, bleating, churning the mud, goats with bright blue markings. Ira consulted the map, made a mental note to look for two wrought stone doors, catacombs. He passed the straggling goats, picked up speed, began to whistle *Amazing Grace* braced by a flood of courage and strong conviction, to dot his i's and cross his t's, to fill in blanks three across (eight letters) the third letter an i, his only clue. The bastards knew the missing letters. He would ask. The bastards. A microscopic swarm of gnats brewed in his ear. Eli's map took him on a game of hide-and-seek with the path through the Carmelite monastery. It was lunchtime by the time he found the dump. Because of the downpour, the narrow path above the house had turned to mud. He was ravenous. His key fit once again but Shechina had blocked the door with metal poles.

It's lunchtime, she informed him through the tiny speak-way, then snapped it shut.

But I'm the son! Don't I get lunch?

Was the son making fun of her? Shechina wondered, unblocking the door. She hung her head at the sight of his sly face as he brushed past straight toward his parent's room. She'd drawn their curtains, retrieved and re-piled Vera's patience cards, including those that had fallen onto the floor. She followed him, watched as he spread lip-gloss on his dry lips and sat at the foot of their bed, his arms, head and legs dangling at various angles. He grabbed a pad of paper, tore off a sheet and rigged up a fever chart. At intervals, Shechina took their temperatures and Ira registered the numbers on his chart. Though the curtains were drawn, clusters of newly born blue-bottle flies crept underneath the fabric, crawled up and down the walls and windowsills, hovered quietly above the old gaping mouths from which sweet vaporous breath seeped in odorous puffs. Between puffs, the flies explored their parched blue lips, Eli's beard an inviting crawl-maze. The notations on the chart were steady at first, then Vera's temperature spiked. Ira wrapped his fingers around the thin skin of her fragile ankle. Though his hand was not strong, he could easily have snapped her bones with it.

Ira carefully squeezed, declaimed, I'm your handful of sperm, your grit in the oyster.

When Ira released Vera's ankle, his hand was briny. He wiped it across the knee of his jeans, swatted intrusive flies that scattered briefly then reassembled. Eli's temperature sank so Ira grasped his arteriosclerotic shoulder. Even at death's door, Eli was dapper, self-assured, his decisive forehead a polished brass plate. The cat woke, stretched, licked her paws and slept again. The whippets slept on, pungently smelling of dog. Ira hoped Shechina would offer lunch. When he crept to the door of the kitchen to see, she was brushing breadcrumbs into a pile on the twenty-year-old lemon-striped oilcloth. At the sight of the kitchen, steeped in cravings, he bristled with hunger and malice. He was tethered to this house now, to the service he had come to provide.

He slunk back toward the deathwatch but veered into Eli's studio instead, breathing in the virile odor of strong paint. Eli's odor, Eli's ardor, unnoted by posterity, undiscouraged by sixty years of oblivion. He gazed at his favorite painting, the map of *Hotel Lutetia* painted on a small three by five canvas (1952). About the painting his mother had confided, I was a most accomplished pianist before the war. One small bit of information gleaned. Also, another crumb revealed: After the war I no longer played but did pipe work and sold off bogus Jan van Goyan landscapes to keep us going. With the proceeds I bought coal, bread, oil, paint, canvas, not in that order and pipe fittings, of course, cigarettes and, finally (1957), peppermint liqueur again. Was that the story? He recalled more: Only cold cash blew away our DP dilapidation. But, Marigold, I doubt you remember postwar, only Cold War? Had there really been pipes and liqueur sipping, long evenings in the French language viewed from his own room (now a tiny room) where Ira once sat in bed cleaning flug from between his toes, cracking his knuckles? (Forbidden by Vera.) His knuckles now ached in damp weather, Vera had been right. He recalled lying on his back and hearing Vera call Eli tactless, had thought, at the time, tact meant tack as in *thumb*. How could I have been so stupid? Of course Vera meant more to him then he did to her. Of course he meant less to either of them than they did to each other.

Their cat stood at the door smelling him disdainfully. This cat had the marbled eyes of a cold-hearted fortune teller. Eli's shelves were lined with a collection of liquor miniatures, also an empty heliotrope bottle of *eau de cologne*. These shelves were Venetian red, the wood floor was sienna and was coated with many layers of varnish. The seat of Eli's yellow kitchen chair held a linseed tin, a plate of buttered toast (old and putrefied) with dried carmine-plum marmalade on top. There were burnt wooden matches left by Vera on her frequent visits to smoke while she looked down her nose at his brush. The bookshelves were chockablock with Eli's brown, illustrated, two-vol-

ume encyclopedia of (*déjà vu*) Victorian pornography.
These volumes had been Ira's introduction to repro-
duction and sex positions. He passed the back of his
hand across his nose. Stripes of pink smeared his
knuckles, his first nosebleed in thirty-five years. He
picked up Eli's sapphire ring from among coins and
peanut husks, walnuts and charcoal bits, and tried to
squeeze it onto his finger. Since all his fingers, including his pinkie, were slug-white and frankfurter-sized,
the ring wouldn't go on. He licked it instead. Blood
pushed in and out of his nostril when he breathed.
He opened the encyclopedia to Oriental Sex Positions, blew into a tissue, gazed at the smear of bloody
threads. He treated himself to a quick wank with his
back to the door, pressing his tongue against his palate. Quickly, a gasp rolled out and bounced off the
wall. He entered the kitchen, plunged both hands
into the soapy-water-filled yellow plastic bucket in
the marble sink. He dried his hands on the green and
ivory flowered apron hanging from a hook. Standing
his tube of lip gloss on the tabletop, he scooped the
last of the breadcrumbs from the little pyramid at
the corner of the oilcloth.

In the bedroom, Vigilante leaped across cres-
cent-shaped black whippets and nestled between two
sets of shatterable hips. At that moment, with a pop,
Vera unstuck her lips, tearing bits of lip skin. Her
body temperature was so hot the cat left the room.
The morphine was wearing off and her limbs were

beginning to twitch. She threw off the eiderdown revealed that the orange petroleum jelly had yeastily oozed everywhere. Her torso in old age began at her neck, ended at her knees. Her teeth chattered and she shivered. Natural grace pressed against her unyielding spine. She thought: Messenger, bring money, please! My dowry! Bring a stick in the mud as a token of his love. From her throat came the caw of a muffled crow as a ghost-crow flew out of her mouth unheard except by the whippets who rose up on their front paws, turned spirals, banged against Eli like gate-crashers. Eli's body yielded but gave no response. His fist remained frozen around the tightly rolled wad of cold cash, as Vera's eyes seeped tears.

In the garden, the cat chased a grasshopper, caught it, tore off one leg. The cat chewed round and round as though it were a chicken bone and tossed it aside then darted toward the kitchen where tinned milk waited in a ceramic bowl while the disabled grasshopper grasped a geranium stalk. The grasshopper blended with the stalk whose leaves were yellow from over-watering, whose dried crimson flower was long overdue for dead-heading. The lopsided grasshopper flew onto a green shutter much in need of sanding and repainting. Could it live out its life missing a leg? From a distance, the grasshopper watched the cat dig sharp claws into the shutter and leap past the kitchen window, dashing through the house into the bedroom and under the bed. The cat batted at Eli's stash of rolled canvasses, also at a half glass of juice (blood orange) and a wadded-up plain white dress.

In concert when the clock radio (timed to wake them for lunch) clicked on, Vera's frown lines (glabellars), crow's feet (periorbitals), acne scars, marionette lines (oral commissures) and deep smile lines (nasolabial furrows) struck up a tune. The radio reassured: The weather is expected to improve. Attica will be cloudy. Temperatures in Athens will range from seven to sixteen degrees Celsius, forty-five to sixty-one Fahrenheit. Thessaloniki cloudy with temperatures between four and thirteen degrees Celsius, thirty-nine and fifty-five Fahrenheit. Eastern Macedonia, Thrace, the Aegean Sea islands, Crete and the Dodecanese cloudy with rain and local storms but the weather will gradually improve. Vera tossed. The eiderdown fell away and her charred nightgown slipped down revealing *f* holes of a violin tattooed in black across her shoulder blades. Finally, soft metronomic breathing resumed and she relaxed, sighed, groaned, snoozed. In the distance the noontime bell tolled as large clouds crept across the sun, causing the horizon to marble. The melodic, tolling village bell (*toque de agonia*) marked the approach of death. Ira stood three rooms back against the kitchen table when he heard the death bell. He visualized death's droll march, saw a blue replica of a church in Rome, heard slow tolling. He experienced curiosity about Tony's Catholic funeral, then, a jolt of inspiration. He reached back to grasp his full quiver of unshot

intentions, found, and disregarded regret and un-
sharpened points. Not to eat game pie with them for
lunch! The recipe, his gift, folded in his wallet. A few
of the blanks in his life's crossword caught his attention – four down, eighteen across, an unruly child,
twenty-seven down, twenty-eight across, undistin-
guished, narrow scope, thirty-six across, eighteen
down, idleness.

It was a relief when the sun (now obscured) no
longer burnt through the window. The odor –
smoked meat. A must, to say, *Goodbye*, say *Merci*, maybe *Gesundheit*. When Ira pulled the refrigerator door
open, he spied a slab of cold game pie on a china
saucer. When the bell tolled somber tones he forgot his resolve and impaled the pie with his tongue.
In three swallows what remained was inhaled. So,
his gift wouldn't have been a surprise after all. Go!
Say goodbye. Go. Quickly. Ask. Am I from where?
Come from what? Whom? The group? The catego-
ry. Classification? The clime? Were our roots pulled
out and by whom? Have they atrophied? Has earth
been shaken off? Birdsong joined the last bell toll. A
smear of cold grease shone on his chin as he fished
in his pocket for change to feed the turnstile. The
cat leapt up and licked the game-imbued crumbs.
Cheshire-like, she rested on her haunches in a sentry
pose, licking furiously. Ira's arms were limp, the ap-
erture (lunchtime) tottered, squeezed shut, the mitral
valve sputtered. Roused by another onset of bells he

dropped a coin into the turnstile, pushed through to the corridor. Though sudden fatigue wrestled him into a chair, he popped back up. Were they dead yet?

Dashing down the hallway into the bedroom, he looked down at Eli and Vera and hadn't a clue. He reached up and grasped the folded beaver-trimmed spread atop their ghastly teak armoire, setting it on a chair stacked with shoeboxes. he removed the remaining change from his pocket, undid the jeweled poniard and dropped everything onto the night table. Next, he pulled off the cowboy boots, peeled away cashmere dun-colored (once brown) socks like orange rinds and stuffed them into the hourglass boots. The moist, callused soles of his feet crunched shards of something. The feet were gnarled like a Dutch poplar. He cringed, shoved a dog rump aside. An influx of sunlight having disentangled from a clutch of cloud-gloom poured across the room. Ira ducked under it and stepped onto the bed. He pressed a space open between his parents, sank onto his knees and squeezed under the eiderdown between them, pulling the heavy spread across all three. The dogs rose up and left the room. The spread felt like a cement slab, its mildew odor overpowered the smell of lamb. Ira hadn't removed his leather jacket with three passports jammed deep into a pocket. Jutting out his profile, his arms were stiff as cobblestones, his legs long oars. Vera was a paddle, Eli a punt pole. Without conviction, sleep stood aside. Their skeletal bodies poked him. He gazed at the henna and copper ceiling, at the moss molding that hung loosely along the south wall. No cherub flew through the room. He concentrated on horizon, close up a mosaic of beaver hairs, far off a square window. Nothing he saw was empty, unmapped, unframed. His eyes moved from one thicket to the next, again surfing the horizon. He squeezed his hand under his belt, into elasticized cotton Jockey shorts. With the nail of his index finger, he searched.

Pa. Ma. Am I Jewish, he queried?

No.

The reply came not from far away at all. Eli and Vera sat up.

No, you're not.

He felt relief but also disappointment.

Then I'm not Jewish?

No. You're not Jewish.

I'm not?

No.

So that was that. He could lay down his sword and shield.

But. You're not not Jewish either, Ma added and gasped.

How to help them? Five hundred milligrams of clorithromycin. Two pills swallowed after eating like a truncheon digging into dense fog. Also Ocean (sodium chloride with benzyl alcohol as a preservative, buffered and made isotonic with sodium bicarbonate) sprayed in a stream at dry nasal membrane. Two Aleves (naproxen sodium) for sinus, thumb and molar pain. This is how Ira helped himself. Also lemon, garlic, seaweed against cancer. Whichever remedy Ira offered, they dismissed, even sneered.

You pay money for saltwater? Vera mocked, swallowing capsules with orange juice, eyeing his plastic squeeze-bottle of Ocean.

Hurry, inching snail, Vera nagged Eli, as he signed his name to a map in cobalt violet.

Eli had on the dark blue seaman's hat that was pulled across one eyebrow. He grabbed a clean canvas, was nibbling little hot peppers, popping them between his lips.

Eli barked, Beer!

Ira leaked tears when Vera shot back, Shut up! Not one of us has cancer.

Music? Ira suggested.

We don't listen to Weill or Hindemith or the puppet Shostakovich anymore, do we Mama? Mama and I—Ira noticed (and didn't like) that Eli called Vera Mama—snack on Mozart and Strauss. Isn't that right, Mama?

Eli's stared at Ira as if he were an *objet trouvé*. His eyes moved over to his wife's face, saw that Vera had stripped down. She wore size five black bra, slip, and panties. Her pipe-cleaner thighs gushed skin folds, the ribs were outlined against silk (nylon?) revealing sentimental bones. The silk (nylon?) quivered as Vera stared back into Eli's butterscotch eyes, his tyrannical dilated pupils. She made no reply.

Mama and I never listen to *Aida* anymore, pallbearer.

Ira let the idea of music capsize, suggested instead, making a flamboyant gesture with his arm, Spicy food?

A beige crocheted doily flew off her dresser when he did so. Vera ravened, poked him with a fleshless, dexterous finger. Get Papa a peach. Cut it away from the pit, a *bris* first.

Eli laughed, poked Ira, She's funny.

Eli held onto the bedpost.

I buy her underwear at Saks. I keep, have always kept, will always keep, her sizes in my wallet.

As the room filled with charcoal-gray steam, Eli declaimed to his wife, Lenin's maternal grandfather was a pious Jew. They've never never never admitted it and never will.

He was winded.

Ira injected, Wasn't Kafka? Charlie Chaplin? Freud too?

Eli swiped the palm of his hand like a machete through the air, accused his son, Platitudes! You know I'm an unbeliever. Why don't you drive *me* into the sea?

Ira chose two peaches from the tree, wiped them on his shirt as he walked into the kitchen and opened an Entenmann's Crumb Cake, breaking off a powdery chunk. With his Swiss army knife he sliced into a soft peach, sectioning it. His fingertips tingled – it seemed a calamity. Nebulous, maybe, but worrying nonetheless, Eli's irony and satire no longer had the old flavor for him. Ira ate dry crumb cake, the taste unchanged after thirty years. From the bedroom he heard squawking of gulls but stayed rooted to the kitchen, eating crumb cake standing up. Forgive, forget. Fleeting time. Uncurated gums. Tartar built along the gum line while he leaned against the calendar that hung from a tack. The hour struck inside his shirt. His boots were half-stuck to the checkerboard linoleum floor. When his lately leaden tortoise-head (potato?) awakened he licked the dusting of powdered sugar from his lips. There were shakes of dry salt and pepper clover scattered on the counter beside vegetables stacked on the oilcloth. More vegetables were piled on the refrigerator and on the van Gogh chair – string beans, violet doodads, ocher with inlaid mother-of-pearl, sandy spinach leaves perched on top of Vera's mottled tortoiseshell eyeglass frames. One of its temples had caved in under the vegetable heap.

He hollered, Shall I boil water in a pot?

He heard Vera's silky voice, Since when can you boil water?

Ira's cheeks blazed. Mustard-colored spots trellised the back of his hands. He leaned against the refrigerator door, had a rueful urge to hold Minx' buttocks in both hands and look at her cranberry-colored ape's anus. I would like to gulp her swollen lips at this very minute, be there, not here. He pictured Minx' furrow, conjured the odor mingling with her hair when she returned from mass – beeswax smoke, incense, unconfusing musks. With his old virtuosity of nose-blowing, he blew into the striped dishtowel, wondered, Who will touch or poke me? Whose slippery epithelial cheeks will hold it? He puzzled over the raw vegetables. Shall I peel cucumbers, introduce myself to radishes, red peppers, tomatoes or peas. Shall I befriend the lonely cauliflower or peal lumpen proletariat potatoes? From the bedroom came the sound of Eli's feeble, biting, sarcastic speechifying, dampening his erogenous ember. He felt flat earth under his feet, anticipated a declamation. He lingered, stroking his tyrannical peepee, making pointillist strummings with his fingertips. Unable to comport himself otherwise, he palmed a slimy peach chunk and rubbed it clockwise (as if he were juicing a lemon) until the carping voice of Eli warbled against the current, switched it to off. How to help them? He composed himself, gathered potatoes, dropped them into a water-filled pot. But how to light it? A match was struck beside him. In a lime green and salmon Djellaba Vera held onto his pants loop and lit the gas.

Mashed! she declaimed, locking his Einstein eyes with hers. You're flushed. Why?

His pallor deepened.

You're the spit image of my Zaiyde. Does *she* make you tapioca?

Who?

Her. This one.

No one makes tapioca.

That's what you think. So why are you flushed?

Ira had no reply.

Do your eyes hurt? Vera asked.

No, but I can't read without glasses anymore. Mashed. A good idea, Ma.

Shush. Eli doesn't need glasses, hears everything too. Where do *we* get our strength?

She coughed.

Weren't you talking about me? asked Ira.

An ablutionary urge like a flying kite weltered up. Ma, remember the stairway we climbed? Remember the black skates?

Shush.

Vera strained at his belt hook, asked, So, why is the loudmouth quiet? I remembered to feed you, did I not? You never went hungry. Tu tu.

She spat green spittle into the pot of cooking potatoes. Shakily, she filled a glass with tap water.

Take it in to him. Do something for once. For him, for once.

She pulled the loop toward the broom closet, told him, Lower the flame, your water's boiling.

Sparks shot from her finger when she touched the brass doorknob. Ira felt staccato current darted from the finger hooked through his pant loop. It jolted his diamond-hard liver, caused his palate and taste buds to tingled. He balanced the water glass while steadying Vera whose eyes were on the bright bulb, attitudinizing. When the whippets squeezed into the hallway, strong as dray horses, Vera steadied herself by gripping one whippet's bony rump.

Carbon, she told Ira, Met oxygen. Also hydrogen. They fell in love. Before marriage they coupled as charcoal. After marriage they coupled as diamond, as graphite. Useful graphite, useful diamond. Remember this story? How many hundreds of times did I tell it to you?

He didn't. He thought instead: A wreath. A plaque. A bunch of red carnations. Does she want acerbity for acerbity? What does she want?

She must have been thinking the same thing. asked, What is it you want, darling?

I want margarine and bagels, calibrated sliced onion.

Still balancing on the dog's rump, she bobbed corklike.

A new lump. Feel here.

She grabbed hold of three of his sausage fingers. Feel the swellings.

She pressed them under her arm. Feather-soft underarm hair brushed his fingertips.

Feel.

Ira was afraid to press, afraid of a tragedy but when she pushed his fingertips downward he felt a shoot like an asparagus tip. Immediately taciturn, he withdrew his hand, used the same fingers to draw her up.

He cooed like a contented pigeon, She makes *witte goud* (white gold) asparagus not tapioca, Ma. She makes it the Dutch way, boiled, with melted butter and cooked ham.

He had her interest.

… with chopped hard boiled eggs, new potatoes.

Eh. Ha. In Holland then?

No I'm …, he couldn't say we, … beside massifs and red porphyry rock.

Ira conjured their vista of heather, lavender, broom, myrtle, cork and oak, their blowing chestnut trees. He wanted to cry.

France? she guessed.

She raised her voice for Eli to hear her, It's estérel, Maures, that's where he's been, making *poésie ron-ron* (purring poetry) with … God knows who. She lowered her voice, Did you feel it?

Yes.

I wasn't kidding.

The rash crawled entirely up his spine to the back of his neck. Why stay? Why forego agave and pine, orange and lemon blossoms? Would Minx wait? Vera walked across the room like a show horse, her knees stiff.

She gibed, Why ruin good asparagus with so much crap?

She grabbed the doorframe, pulled herself inside the bedroom, began adjusting the tower of shoeboxes on the chair. Ira was right behind.

We cook asparagus upright so they hold the flavor. We cover the saucepan with a linen cloth.

Mama makes the best! Eli bragged.

We add sugar, a lump of butter, salt and pepper, cook it three minutes, let it cool, then cook it again for five minutes. This way it flushes out his impurities, detoxifies him, improves potency. Try it like that. Tell *her* how to do it right. You forgot his sliced peach.

The dewlap under her throat hung pendulously.

Ira was blank, so Vera intoned again in a dulcet voice, Peach.

Her dewlap shook as she turned on the overhead light illuminating unhygienic encrustations, also Eli's beakish profile elongated by the runway beard. Ira picked up a fork coated with dried paste of garlic, licked the prongs, inserted it down the neck of his black jersey and began to scratch north to south. Steadying herself, Vera walked back along the dusty-rose wallpaper toward the kitchen, retraced her steps, high stepping, called, Mashed or hot potato salad?

Ira laid his palm on Eli's bony shoulder, Is there charcoal, Papa? Shouted, Mashed, Ma. I already said so.

Charcoal's on the window sill where it's been for a hundred years, Eli told him.

The overhead light flickered. A cluster of charcoal and colored chalk bits, burnt matchsticks, were strewn on the windowsill. Also on the windowsill, a cap made of glossy brown marten fur with earflaps. Ira picked up a piece of charcoal the size of the nail on his pinkie and ate it, staring at Eli's bent back. There was a hissing noise like a hot coal or a snake. Volts of will passed back and forth between son and father.

Eli carped, That so-called peach.

The so-called peach, thought Ira, a diarrhea time-bomb ticking.

Dad, mind if I lie down?

Lie down? Lie down in sheep dip. Since when do you have to ask?

Mama, Eli called out, his tongue flicking, He's forgotten what we're like. He mustn't remember our cherry tree and swallowing the pits.

Eli loomed above his son's face.

Back up, back off, Dad.

Ira's hair and neck were soaking. He stretched out across their bed. One whippet lifted itself to look. Eli struggled with a roll of heavy brown paper, stumbled backwards, commented, The moon kept me awake all night, those damned clucking chickens.

His ribs stuck out as he strained to cut the paper with a single-edged razor blade. Ira smelled seaweed, saw streaks of carmine in the visible sky.

He's yellow, Eli broadcast to the strong smell of garlic that entered the room bringing Vera in its wake carrying a wicker tray laden with garlic-laced mashed potatoes done as no one else in the world could, also a bowl of sliced peaches.

My rabid dogs, she enthused, shakily lowering the tray onto the bed. Put down that butcher paper. Eat.

You eat.

You eat. I ate in the kitchen standing up.

Ira propped himself against three pillows, dipped his fork into Mount Garlic. Supervising with one intercepting eye, Vera jabbed his shoulder blade with rapid pixels of command.

Take off that hot jacket.

He heard thumping sounds.

I'm sweltering just looking at you, Vera rolled her eyes with fugal drama.

Ira addressed the whippets: When *she's* hot, I'm supposed to take off my jacket? *He* talks to me like I'm not here.

Enough manifesto, Eli dictated through beard hair.

Eli held onto the windowsill and slipped a plastic bag over his head.

See what you made him do, Ira G.

Eli braced against the green shutters, spoke through the plastic, Go ahead, eat the rest, I'm not hungry.

Vera enjoined, It's you that needs the edible vaccine, Marigold. Let me see.

Vera shook down the thermometer, a thin rod, six centimeters long. She inserted the electrode into a small hole in his frontal lobe without interrupting his chewing. When three minutes had passed, she removed it, held the rod in the air while casting around the bedside table for her glasses. Not finding them, she nudged Eli.

Read the thermometer.

Eli removed the plastic from his head, crumpled it, answered, It's not normal.

How high? Ira asked.

It's not high, it's low.

Ira covered both ears with the palms of his hands and composed a postcard: *Dear Minx. Clogged pores. Pineal shut down. Lead in my wings. This is to express my penitential contrition. Of course, I angled and overshot the mark. Am in Egypt. Yr. I.* He swallowed the last peach then peeled away his jacket, sleeve by sleeve. Pearl-shaped bubbles formed at the corners of his mouth. He watched Eli doodling jocular overlapping hammers and sickles with sand-colored chalk while doting on his wife's rutted face. Whenever she moved or puttered, folding Ira's jacket, adjusting a stray hair, lighting a shaky match for the next cigarette, as Vera paced in front of her son, smoking nonstop, Eli kept her under surveillance. He sat at the foot of the bed in Jockey shorts watching a thin icy crust form around his good son's neck, encasing the carotid arteries. Ira's face radiated imbecilic contentment, his sad eyes opened as his lips closed. His lap was freezing up as a squirt of diarrhea shot out of its own accord. *Best foot forward*, Minx had advised just before departure while they'd stood beside the fountain. *They'll take pity*, she'd promised while rocking, arms around each other. When the train came, its wheels shot sparks. Above them, pale phosphorescence with red clouds bringing evening. They'd huddled, discussed the train schedule, struck chord after chord. Ira knew twenty words of French, twenty-five words of Greek, ten words of Spanish, four words of Russian, as well as visceral Italian. What he didn't know, Minx translated while Ira counted out coins, his heart stuffed into his mouth. He knew five words in German plus counting from one to nine, taught by Vera: *eins, zwei, drei, vier, fünf, sechs, sieben, acht, neun*. The skin on Vera's hand was discolored now, hadn't been then. Both parents were receptive to the irascible current in Ira's yellow-ocher forehead.

Eli challenged him, Be a *mensch*.

Then Eli scribbled a preposterous khaki copy of Rembrandt's *Three Crosses* on a clean page in his sketchbook, tore it out and held it up in front of his son's face.

✦

There were ebulae, asteroids and craters on the surface of his brain, also orbiting dust, a hazy mass, a stringy growth from boasting. There were croaking tadpoles of angry matter, also, cays of smudged snow crystal. The mapped ancestry (*yichus*) had frozen (*far-*

froyren). Also: A lump of sugar (*shtik tsuker*), one summit reached. This summit was rosette-shaped with
a bulging crust. The brain terrain closely hugged
swollen autoerotic quasars. One time Diedier, his
French barber, told him that his cranium was spotted with freckles. An unusual occurrence. Since he'd
never seen his own cranium, he didn't know wheth-
er to believe him. To the touch, his skull felt like a
medium-well-cooked porterhouse. It was a bald disk
surrounded by a gray-veined halo of brown curls
fenced in by red, out-turned ears that easily filled
with water. The upper lip and chin had the texture
of sandpaper. His smile was shaped like a sardine.
He had scratched the rash once too often and left
khaki scabs. His only expertise (acquired at age thirteen while camping with Tony) was that he could
make a perfect envelope (klondike) bed: Flat poncho.
The first blanket—one edge folded down the center
of the poncho. The second blanket—one edge in the
middle also folded down. Alternate blankets—in the
same way. Sheet folded in half, placed in the middle.
Starting with the last blanket, with Tony's help, take
folded blankets, alternate in reverse order until all
were folded over the middle. Fold poncho over. Snap
together. Put pajamas and toilet articles inside.

Ira had been the one who rolled their envelope
bed down from the bottom, Tony stayed still. At
night they'd wriggled down, didn't disrupt, didn't
turn over, slept side-by-side on pine needles looking
up at the stars through slats in the tree even when

rain swept everything in sheets. Giddy always with his first friend, he had fewer inhibitions with Tony. Their favorite campsite named *bourgeois swamp* by Eli. He and Tony had chipped in for a boy's-sized axe – half-pound head, twenty-four-inch-long handle. Tony read the enclosed instructions out loud while Ira followed them. He held the axe in both hands, right hand with palm under the handle at the head, left with palm over at the end. Is this right, Tony? He tried swinging it at the log on the ground after Tony put his foot on the end of the log to keep it steady. Weight must be even. Ira counted, One, two, three. He raised the axe-head with his right hand. Tony read: Left hand moves up and a little to the front. No. Not so much. Bend your elbows. Let your right hand slip down the handle to the other hand. The head of the axe fell. Ira tried to train his eyes where he expected to hit. As the axe fell, he straightened his elbows. Not so stiff, Tony told him. The axe bit into the log. Ira swung again, his eyes on Tony's foot instead of the spot. It's not a cleaver. Tony pointed to the black oak. I'll try that when it's my turn. He'd removed his foot from the log. Tony swung. The log had jumped up. Vera referred to Scout Tony as Scout *Nudnick.* Why forty-nine steps? Why not forty-eight or fifty? Why defilement? Who helps me? Why map my brain, Dad? Why no patina? The coil pattern in my brain matter, is it from Ma or from Pa? Will it grow dark gradually? Or, all at once at the end? Having already experienced dendritic drainage, worship of goose-down, he hoped that before it happened, Jericho would learn to play the xylophone and Minx might serve as a footstool. Perhaps. And, oh yes, Barbara…

Eli ranted as if he were at the Bund. Vera over-cautioned, pushed something pointed into Ira's brain tissue again and explained, A violin is more respected than a drum, a cello more than a trumpet.

Icy crust continued creeping down to his lumpen knees. Noctambulistic by nature, pen in hand, Vera studied their forty-nine stocks, made notes, glasses sliding down the bridge bone. An uneasy index finger pushed the glasses back up. Eli made fanciful sucking noises to dislodge the food stuck between gums and bridge. Their *proste yiden, shayne yiden* loomed – enlarged hands folded. Eli couldn't have reached around his son's papaya pink, frozen girth if he'd tried. With unusual tenderness, Eli pursed his lips into a keyhole shape that he brought close-up to Ira's eye.

You'll embarrass him, Vera warned.

Ira's lazy optic nerve arched cat-like, an ice web, an *elan vital*. The web covered corneal clusters too. Eli breathed out lilac, was buttonholed by fingers gripping his jersey. Indelible cerulean veins rivered Vera's wrist, her furtive fingers clasped the pen that marked bond issues for a secure future. The orgasm (horizontal, coppery) began to metastasize but got stuck in his spongy calves. The worn tortoise retracted its head, had bitten off all that it could. The spangled image of Minx curled away, tomato-red hair gone limp. Ira reconsidered her polka-dot warts, especially the one beside the epithelial scar and the sad swatch of psoriasis. He supposed that Minx read his letters, tossed them into a film can afterwards then rose up to sort broccoli, cauliflower and cabbage on the kitchen table. Oh vegetables – olive green, fern green, brawny white. Ira anticipated a gaseous violet ice cloud *post coitus* if only his parents would leave the room and take their pets too.

While Eli stood above his good son, geysers of ice and gas spurted against his face. Wispy clouds of white (snow) swirled like a gathering storm. Eli grabbed for Vera's cranium but clasped only her glasses. Mama! he gasped, went white and crumpled. Vera's bonds faded out of focus when the glasses leaped from her nose. She looked up, watched her husband's death, so poignant she caught her breath, applauded resoundingly by way of ovation. Has it ended? She lit a shaking cigarette, smoked it, inhaled though it had no taste and burnt the tip of her tongue, was not even faintly lilac-flavored. The cat leapt across Eli's head, dashed out of the room. Eels swam across Vera's retina. She could smell the strong perfume of jealousy. Why him? Why not me? The sucked cigarette gave consolation. Why no lilac? She could make out colored mustards through the window, could faintly hear chiming church bells. She smoked the cigarette down to sepia, dashed its end into the bedside bowl against jade and khaki bits and pieces.

G'vald. I didn't cook enough prime rib. Not enough sirloin...

She smacked Eli's face.

What about the suicide pact? *Umzist.*

Vera prodded Eli sharply with her finger. Shards on eyes? Yes or no? Stem of myrtle between your fingers? Ah those fingers! Yes or no?

Yes and no, she ruminated. We had one Neanderthal, and one Marigold. How Marigold hated the nickname. But, we unfailingly used it when he wore that famous guilty smirk.

The life-sized block of ice with Marigold's smudged smirk frozen in sepia (an Olitski landscape with two eyes, eyebrows, a tall forehead) pierced both of their old hearts. She spoke to it: Carp or herring, Ira? Did your friends think I was Mommy or Oma?

She bit into her devoted lead pencil, left marks in the canary-yellow wood. She strained to see Eli's cadaverous face—Old Long Since—O.L.S.

Without maggots please, without spittle. That's what *I* want. Those are my wishes.

Vera removed the skin-colored brassiere that didn't match her black cotton panties. Her old fingers were beleaguered by nylon and clips, yellow pencil, minutiae foul and incomplete. She veered like a vagrant against the bed frame, stumbled over

Eli's foot until the whippets crowded against her, pushed her into the dolphin-tail chair. The cat stayed back, lurked in the doorway. Shoeboxes came un-balanced, two spilled. Out rolled a bow tie of black patent leather and two pumps. Minutes spilled wil-ly-nilly from the shoebox onto which Vigilante leapt, pushing it entirely over with her cold nose in order to hunt inside the tissue paper for reds long hidden. Also in the crawl space were hollow clay pigeons and, in the pocket of his double-breasted suit, a vel-lum date book. By leaning over, Vera could look into Eli's sockets that had leaked spittle (foam?). She saw a brittle human face, an upturned wizard's beard.

The electric light burned because daylight was pallid. There had been some drizzle earlier. Eli's knees were at right angles doing no harm. His bis-cuit-colored, cherub's feet were honey-combed with white blotches. Escaping minutes swarmed over him. Beady, rapid, they rushed into his nostrils. Octopole strands of minutes rolled down both sides of his mud-dy neck ricocheting against silent bacteria and chest-nuts. Vera's inky fingertips were pitched in prayer while her hieratic hands cupped bee bee-hard min-utes that dripped into the cup of flesh. Vera pulled at her stockings (stretching silken bands) until, one by one, she pulled them away from her sticky toes. She searched for the pink quilted robe, forgetting that it had been given away to Hadassah Thrift Shop thir-ty years before. She searched through both closets, couldn't remember where she'd left it. Is it drying on the rope my unhandy husband stretched between the two cherry trees? She warily leaned closer to look at her dead husband. Her eyes overflowed unstoppably when she bent toward the performance. Holding onto the scaffolding/bed frame she totaled the years. Yes, nearly seventy years without egg, shank bone, or bitter herbs.

G'vald. She kicked at his corpse, *Olreitnik*. We wasted the flu shot.

A wound, where she had kicked, opened. She turned and also kicked at her son encased in an ice block whiter than milk. Kill a red spider and seventy-seven sins would be forgiven. She kicked her *treyf possl* (unfit and forbidden) again.

Please, Ira, tea and jam, a *nashn, beygl, beygeleh*.

Her leg trembled. She reached for a fresh cigarette, a match, lit the match. Eli's mocha, not dead, lips started to ripple in slow tempi. She saw an unobservant moving Jew whose mouth was filled with living XY nucleic acid. His lips were again cavalier, his blackbird eyes reopened.

Eli valorized, whispered, Not seventy, sixty-five years with the same sunflower.

Eli reached out and stroked the blue cloud, asked her, Did you swing from my beard?

His wife appeared far off, a hovering hummingbird. She saw that he truly was not dead, was not a mongoose, had not a drop of oil in his hair.

✦

Vera's white arms touted eighty thousand genes hanging like tennis rackets. She and her husband were standing above their son when geysers of ice and gas shot against their faces. Tangled clouds of ice and snow churned like a storm. Vera grabbed for Eli's beard. His oversized tongue rolled out as he tried to snare her hand.

She asked, How can we help our rhinoceros?

Eli grasped three of her fingers, steadied her. He held anise suckers in his hand.

Would oil help?

Scruffy, Vera commented, taking a closer look at the ice block.

Receptor genes stuck out their little tongues at Vera. She strained to look into the pupils of her son's eyes for any frontal-cortex activity but could see none since ice drizzle covered his eyeballs too. Snow had accumulated along his forehead, on the bridge of his nose and on his cheekbones. Discouraged by their son's condition, Eli's knees sagged as if in a swoon. He braised himself when he rose halfway and leaned against her, his cheeks like soft blue figs, his gamey breath causing her hair to flutter. *Klaineh kinder lozen nit shlofen; groisseh kinder lozen nit ruen.* (Small children don't let you sleep; big children don't let you rest.) Vera steadied Eli, his effulgent mother too. She ransacked for old strength having wasted an obituary, the ink not dry. She steadied him while uncaring cells

quivered through her. She smoothed her son's gray-
ing hair with the same hand.

What a *haimish ponimel!*

One whippet begged, while the other lay down
and played dead. Ever cynical, Vera gathered wild
plants, weeded around the funky carpet, finding
breadcrumbs, Cyclops hair, vinegar stains, carniv-
orous droppings, cake, cinnamon, cloves, pimiento. She brushed everything under the bed, joyfully
stalked Eli with a bouquet of wilted stems. Proud
of his swan song, Eli turned his back on her stirring
spirit to pick up his gummy paintbrush. The block's
eugenic epicenter was thawing out, Mendelian peas
that had downsized by high hopes, chafed and la-
bored against Ira's incorrigible opaque personality.
He thought of himself as somewhere between im-
becile and genius, had ungovernable moods, was a
peacock nonetheless. He wore no underpants, had
no capital, was nearing extinction in his second
childhood while his parents patrolled. Eli immured,
had on a hundred-percent cotton pajama top. He
soothed Vera's velvet nervous pets, cramped against
fallen affidavits that had fertilized a trail of spruce.

Queasy, Ira? Can you hear us?

Ira's stomach gurgled its compendious contents of
rinds of ideology, entrapped cultural fat, rapacious,
precocious, cynical beef. His imposition yearned for
rescue. Vera plumped up the pillows, uncorked a bottle of Pinot Noir Reserve and put two stem glasses on

the red and yellow Parcheesi board, first spreading out an orange and black woven coverlet that had a border of prancing horses across his knees. She and Eli could, would, provide palliative care until he revived or died or left for the black lava reef or even the white sandy coastline in headlong Pavlovian pursuit of *her*.

Vera asked Eli with an invigorating shout, Should we provoke our *kinderleck*, all twenty-three pairs of chromosomes?

He wanted an Airedale. Remember so much, Mama? Should we get him one? Is it too late?

Vera combed her son's hair across his forehead, Julius Caesar style. His swollen throat bulged with bacteria. Her lemony voice was loud in his ears. Diluted by lineage, apportioned between parents, the twitching gesture he made by squeezing his eyes was not understood. Eli had an idea, he found his toothbrush, squeezed toothpaste into a shimmering V but stumbled against circumambient forgetfulness before he could test his idea.

He chimed, *Mamishka.* and hollered in a tone of sulphurous irritation, I curse imperialists! I curse the Truman Doctrine! I denounce Glasnost! We were too permissive, Mama.

She gave Eli a bat on the head, said, You're a nuisance. I'm an authority.

She resumed forbearance, didn't panic.

Vera followed Vigilante into the kitchen, taking tiny steps and carried the hot, doughy, loaf of *loiter* bread in the shape of a ladder back. Eli was having trouble pulling his axe and iron chain from under the bed where the toothbrush had fallen. His feet were swelling.

He mumbled, *Chazer* (pig) *ai ai.*

Vera toasted him with wine.

Mazel tov.

God willing, Eli enjoined.

Was the pungent odor their son's feet? His mouth? Was the odor expungeable? It was so strong so uncanny, it had pierced Vera's dim olfactories, had stirred Eli's nasal ganglia.

He shook his fist, Doom to all enemies of collectivization, and pulled his undershirt up to his nose.

Eli took another sniff to be certain as his nose was no longer reliable, no longer a crowning, manly sense.

Eat, Vera insisted.

Jerkily, she poured wine for herself, pinched the bread and began to murmur when she saw unseasonal wet snow falling onto the tiny buds of crocus, daffodil, snowdrops through the window.

Am I a murderer? Vera asked, Our *kleinen buergerlichen* (petit bourgeois) left us for dead. This one didn't, Bubbie, grant him that.

Snow turned into drizzle, then rain, then downpour.

Am I an olive? Am I moronic?

Watching her garden getting soaked, she squeezed closer to Ira's regal silhouette, pulled down the shade. She looked Ira up and down. He had rhododendron ears, like Eli. Karl had pearl ears, like hers.

My uterus, she bragged.

My brush stroke, Eli bragged.

He was nothing like a collision fragment circling the earth evermore, in fact, the ice-bulk was the furthest thing from a *kleinen buergerlichen* (petit bourgeois).

I'm ravenous, she enjoined. She meant to say sweet-heart but said, I'm selfish-heart, instead.

They won't accept help. Have I helped nonetheless? Ira mulled, and decided, I've generated self-help. He watched animal mastication, noticed that Eli's denture was loose. He heard their conversation, though not in any language he understood. He smelled a mean odor. They needed baths, not doctors, not shrouds. His cowboy boots with cashmere socks balled inside stood like two colossi next to the armoire. Arch determination and strong centripetal forces aside, he remained tethered to them as Vera's irritating whippets stepped over his ice-encased legs. In a hurry with herring, Shechina returned from the market and looked in on her old folks. Eli's contextless eyes had closed in on the coverlet's prancing horses while Vera pinched bread and soaked it in seawater. For digestion. Vera saw Shechina's mystified look and explained, I'm not nauseated, just sour. Nor am I despondent. Don't just stand there, Shechina.

With a welter of impending doom, also relief, a crack sounded and the son was able to flex his rude knees. Shechina shirred past the ice-covered ape and forcing up the window allowing the room to be swamped with wet air. Fresh from mass, dripping piety, chastened, Shechina tossed her rain-wet hair as she'd tossed coins into the alms basket, as she too had tossed off all blood bonds and crushed the cocoon with her flat shoe. Shearing dead tulips petals, stems/stamen remaining in the squat vase, Shechina scattered hovering insects that had ridden in on wet air with a slap. Eli's engine purred. Vera began to sort variegated account sheets. Shechina set fuzzy, unwashed peaches on the yellow, drooled-on pillowcase, sallied over to shoo Vigilante (who had crept back in) out. The breeze kicked up sprays of spores, also seeds, stamps, eraser dust. The room backed away from the moist evanescence of natural, mushrooming weather. Shechina whispered in Ira's ear, Parasite! Orbiting her short arms around, she sniped at him again, Dungheap! and crouched to examine dead gardenias and cobblestones. Vigilante preened, neck elongating, sure of the usual reprieve or mercy, licking her fur. A button from Shechina's soaked violet velvet shirt popped when she stood back up, cobblestone in hand. With quivering calves, she navigated a grouchy fandango. She had tiny quivering pomegranate breasts, addled ears, grimy hands, bobbing eyebrows. Eli sometimes called her a guileless crone. The propulsive cat followed Shechina in hope of boiled chicken livers.

✦

Stormy torrent in his chest, gassy reflux gurgling in his gut, the tempest tapered off and soft light suffused into twilight. Ira dropped the red ball back into his KLM bag while side-stepping Vigilante when she flew through the air. Her inky eyes were immune to static electricity, partial to oboes and can openers that pierced indigo tin labels, oblivious to draconian door-slamming. Vera's filigree face was grave, she admitted, Terrible indigestion. Swallowed flies. Feet swollen. I played Schubert before I was ten.

She sat on the chintz chair.

Water, Eli. Celery? I'm sweltering. My hands are cramped. I could sight-read but no more. Camille Saint-Saëns. *You* play Saint-Saëns. You can't. Our child can't. Won't.

She air kissed, up to her wrists in bacteria.

No Great Dane for my son. Clover and grass stains on his red corduroy overalls, *you* get them out. You, my dear husband hated basil. Try cooking without basil for sixty years. Where's my cane, Bubbie?

Percussively, Eli hollered, What cane? Stop with the cane bullshit.

You're faultless and I'm no Medea. I can't joke?

She swatted ethereal green flies bruising their exotic plumage. Eli emulated the rapture, tossed his head against the corrugated iron bedpost. He was an old centurion twisting the flounced duvet. He craned his neck in the direction of Vera's sightline though Vera's eyes were ensnared by his son, captivated by his primitive foot as it pressed into the boot. When his foot disappeared, she moved her panicky gaze onto Eli, demanded insistently, Do something!

The boots felt tight. He swallowed chuckles, had inoculated himself with Salvationist ruses. After ignoring uncombed hair, he changed his mind and smoothed it with his palm, clockwise around the soft scalp. He folded a clean undershirt.

Don't laugh, Pa, she's not pregnant. Should I water your geraniums before I go, Ma? Should I tighten the clothesline between the two birch trees, Ma?

Use your brain, Vera snapped by way of reply.

Does she look like a chaplain? Eli asked, scattering the same flies for the fifth time.

With each gesture, the flies advanced, retreated, advanced. Eli reached for Vera's humped back, palpated the pocket between her shoulder blades, the periwinkle cloth. He studied her hair, when washed it was like springy cashmere. Her hair produced enough current to charge Eli's nerve ends. Her frog hands had the feel of felt. Vera puckered her lips while Ira played an uneasy second fiddle.

Ira posited, Lunch?

Without hindsight, Ira cadged a feel of his crotch. What had it been like? Since he lacked concrete memory to detail much of his unsensational childhood, he wasn't sure.

Are you against euthanasia, Pa? he asked.

Is it allowed here? I didn't think it was, his father replied.

Vera's green turban covered her hair. In his spruce suit (a dry-cleaned scarecrow) Eli squeezed vermilion onto his palette while they waited, stricken. He contemplated the comestibles that Ira had assembled on the wicker tray – kiwi fruit, cheese chunks, round whole wheat crackers, tepid fetishes. Ira was spruced up for the farewell. His nose silted up. He hadn't learned how to prepare paschal roast lamb or singing trout. Vera assuaged him, uttered, Try the cheese, though she was engrossed in fastening earrings.

MOSES, A PAPERWEIGHT

Snelheid, 524 kilometers per verst, Ira watched a crude map of Canada, an arrow burping with Dutch logic across the Hudson Bay. Walled into his seat, a curtain dropped across the pink glow of sunset. Behind the curtain, dark nebulae. His pupils dilated, the creases crossing his forehead smoothed out. Bending forward, twisting his starched neck, he gazed across the neighbor's barrel chest out the tiny window straining for a look into the galaxy. He had on a new red mail-order Basque beret made in the Czech Republic. Hearing a hiss, softly loud, Ira experienced hurtling through space. Exalted crows, good-for-nothings, penised, hovered overhead. He brushed their black feathers with his folded *Herald Tribune* to ward them away. Turbulence took hold of the *Flying Dutchman*. Ira's heart went for an unsynchronized swim. He sensed providential disaster, was undefended, nonetheless faked aplomb. The seatmate dropped coins onto his lap in a monkey ballet off to the WC.

Don't get up, the woman's voice instructed, her heel pressing into the toe of his leather boot. The smell of peony poured from her.

Grenadine, she told the stewardess as she marched back up the aisle almost as soon as she had gone.

Turbulence or not, full bladder or not, with no gravitational grip, the crows mixed in with magenta specks. His seatmate raised a glass and inquired, Buenos Aires or Paris? *Bel esprit.*

Ira clucked, *Oui et oui.*

He cupped his ear, heard, *Prost*, watched amber liquid swallowed. Amoebas henpecked (pecked over) his intestinal wall, shambling in silly daffodil bobbings, creating a furor. The neighbor brushed white hair away from her eyes. Watery fear gurgled during a fierce bout of bullying turbulence. Indeed, the flight had gone sour. For the only time in his life, he yielded to the inevitable impending disaster, resigned himself to scutter needle-sharp over Greenland where he would break up into half a loaf imbedding in snow. The aircraft shook like a whirligig. His balled fist gripped red-lined corduroy (the back pocket mended by Vera). He imagined falling off.

Samson, the woman declaimed, her index finger tapping a *petit point* rapture on his arm.

Ira feigned sleep, spoke to God: Dear God. I am one hundred percent spinning sperm. I have cowering Jewish giblets and a throbbing pulse, also primrose swollen feet and I'm soon to overturn over Greenland. Just kill me now, please. Get it over with!

God, end this ferocious fear caused by your wicked nature. Blinking, sable lashes basted dry cheeks, his mallards throat constricted. The neighbor's fingers sashayed down his thighway, squeezed under his fist, rudely dislodged it, unplugging his drain. She dismissed his reserve with scarlet nails and dug toward his withered vessel and spear. The aircraft made another jittering onslaught downhill at an alarming speed with metallic rustlings and flailings. Ira flinched, quailed and sweated, faked merriment, with teeth bared while the aircraft pin-balled. Miles below lay the distant planet, an ice-way, exorbitant, a self-important Mecca.

Orange and scarlet licks of fire tongued up from under Ira's beret. A sky-blue-suited attendant, Talia G., wearing mauve electrical gloves with tapered fingertips, rushed up the aisle and suffocated ribbony tendrils of flame. Another attendant, Thor G., cracked a plastic porthole that sucked smoke and stench away. Unaccountably, cobalt-blue *eau de cologne* was released. The aircraft steadied, became silent except for the hum of rheumy engines. On the screen, the news crawled by: *The German DAX Index plunged 51.26. In London, the Hundred Share Index dropped 74.1 points. In Paris the CAC 40 Index fell 43.05 points. In Switzerland the Index dropped 92.2 points. In the U.S. the Dow dropped 57.40 points. International sentiment seems to be fragile.* Passengers whistled and shouted. Like it or not, black on white cooking smells seeped into the cabin. Glad travelers snapped up window shades revealing murky white light. Endurance rewarded, Ira unhunched his shoulders. Empty miniature bottles filled his pouch, also half-done crossword puzzles. In-flight magazines had been squeezed behind eight carceral hours of slow death-dose. He didn't remove the navy blue pillow from the crook of his neck. Hovering above, Thor G.'s tray offered echo-laced minerals in ozone.

He urged Ira, Wet your whistle, Little Red.

Ira wiped his face with the hot wet wash cloth being offered, began a long self-inventory in his datebook:

ardor
sepia
heir
strong arms overreaching
thick skin
eat fingernails
red badge
percolating
on feet
pasty jism
mood creature
not wistful
no tattoo
three passports
satiety
riposte
shock

Refolding washcloths, Thor G. spoke in a deprecating tone of the repast on its way: Yogurt, honey, an overstuffed bagel. Oye.

Ira rose, lifted the pink umbilical chain and squeezed down the narrow aisle. He ploughed past a trolley holding Meissen china cups and fresh coffee. He looked into maroon faces. Refreshed after the wash, fear free, Ira made jigsaw plans, a second list:

change money

wear lozenge-patterned sweater

cross-check for Swiss army knife

put fruit into bag

Talia G. passed by, chimed, Orange or lemon? Juice? Or fruit?

Dolefully spruced up to serve breakfast, wearing a fresh gay acid-green scarf, she flashed sugar and spice packets, fresh shirts, red poppy pins, raspberries with and without powdered sugar, kosher and not. Ira followed a large Greek up the aisle. Though not two hours from landing, the aircraft was still climbing at a steep angle, or so it seemed as he strained uphill.

Cocooned in the sweater with bright ocher and salmon diamonds (Barbara's gift), the blanket up to his chin, Ira stretched himself in woolly increments. His feet were numb. He listened to unreliable babblings by birds in Greek, wished that his own fluid ancestry sounded such a gravelly bell. Many-sided accretions of gas along with amino-acid-laced nucleotides built in his blood, felt like heartburn. When

the cluster caused a belch, it diluted, but, soon leav-
ened again, immolated again. His goose-necked
bassoon Messiah, too frugal with relief, rubbed him
(had always rubbed him) the wrong way. Straining
to belch, his lips moved, releasing fish breath (pop-
py-seed bouquet) with a gustatory splash. He spun
the wheel, lifted off his yoke, conjured leg of lamb
but ordered fish soup with lemongrass. He waited,
craned his neck to see if Talia G. was getting close
with the trolley. She was. He could see her toing and
froing with jollity, jockeying tart face-washers, brushing away dragonflies, mayflies and young bees while
handing out trays. There rose up a restorative salty
sea smell. He checked on his money while bacteria
multiplied along his sticky gumline.

Ira shrank from eye contact. He was impatient for
wild white yonder. He submitted to random shutter-
ings, in descent, chunting full flood. When he could
stand up, he packed up plums, good conscience, Vera's yellow diamond wrapped in foil, Eli's ring with
its milky jewel also wrapped in foil. He folded the em-
bellished obituary in with maps, reparation receipts,
cheese, snapshots of whippets and cat and black and
white photographs culled from Vera's trunk. His
mulish hands couldn't squeeze anything more into
the suitcase because it was chockablock with rubber-banded paper currency and grimy certificates.
He rearranged his flight bag (plums first) until he was
forced back into his seat by school children wearing
white sailor suits with pipe trim high-stepping like

show horses in single file. One by one, the children were inoculated by a nurse against ancient culture and cricket song. Then, the children were given stern warnings against refined granulated sugar. The crew distributed lists of gymnasiums. Buttressed by the grind of lowered landing wheels, Ira craved lunch – grilled fish.

His eyes filled but not with tears as the taxi looped fearlessly around clots of dark people causing the decorative wolf's pelt on the rear view mirror to fly onto the front seat against wormy green fruit that had split a brown paper bag. The taxi lifted off the ground, rammed vaporous sunlight. The driver skirted Byzantine fragments of dome, drove down a tiled corridor, out into a light bath. The clock hands (glow-worms) flickered, tripping a diastolic malfunction in Ira's heart, its mandate twigged even the roots of his teeth. The taxi skirted rock-hewn paths, grape vines, fig trees, gray stone buildings with arched windows, brown shrubs, crumbling ultramarine-blue frescoes depicting enactments of miracles. Mandolin and lute music was inserted into the CD player by the driver, the volume loud and honeysuckly sweet/sour. Ira's disfigured heart valves flinched. A fist hammered against his atrophied pecs, then stopped. He felt plausible relief. He was very tired. His pale orange lips were at half-extinguished attention. He didn't recognize the gentle voice that was speaking to him, experienced no premonitions or foreshadowing. Instead he took coins from the small pocket, put them in his big pocket – son to father. The driver deciphered vermilion roadside instructions: penalties, fines. It was thirteen kilometers to the lottery kiosk where an onion with an arrow pointed in the direction they were going. The taxi accelerated when the rusty iron barricade was raised up, then skirted a lemon forest, after that, an olive grove.

Ira's hulking pulmonary artery (an arced vase-like estuary) pumped steadfast, sending bright color into his effecting face. He blinked when the taxi passed vegetables in pyramids, plants that were coded species. Also at the market, shrimp and clams in buckets, whole hams, mushrooms, lemons, carrots, green and red and yellow peppers, chard, spinach, cucumbers, asparagus, grapefruits, oranges, eggs, herring, sardines, stacks of pot holders. The taxi sped through a thick pine-filled ravine past stone hummocks and clumps that once (1,700 years ago) were benches and pedestals for statues. The loud music blotted out songs of owls and crickets. When the taxi rounded onto the final straightaway, the stone clock tower glinted in a ripe sunbeam. It drove past green/silver olive groves carpeted with poppies. Drops of water rolled down Ira's neck into the once-black jersey. He tapped the driver's shoulder.

Slow down!

The driver didn't understand, offered a yellow lozenge that smelled and tasted like eucalyptus. He pitied the sad boy with so much white hair flecking his unshaven, unwashed, carrot-colored cheeks, clasping a key like an arc of covenant. Digressive recollections jogged Ira's thoughts: Promises made. Indignation. Didn't love Ma's cat. Didn't pet. Didn't feed. Forgot to look for Swiss knife. He began another list:

> *was unpliant*
> *was incorrigible*
> *didn't take vitamin supplements*
> *left the ripe cheese in the overhead bin on the airplane*
> *was chilly*
> *had no pity*
> *was top-heavy*
> *didn't refrigerate leftovers*
> *preserved nothing*

His kidney leaked protein into stored urine, nerve cells had been dying since breakfast. Ira smelled perfume. He wondered, Does the driver see me as a spoiled man? Or, does he think I'm middle of the road? The taxi stopped abruptly. Ira flew forward, hitting his front teeth against the driver's hard skull.

O Barbara. Nothing to eat except old pimiento cheese, froglike, ready to spring. Black garbage bags lined the celestial sphere. Ira leaped onto the couch, tossed his flight bag toward a shelf. The couch springs spoke in squeaks. He stepped down, feet splayed on flat earth and unbuttoned the top of his jeans, avoided the third rail. He poured himself a bowl of very cold milk. While sipping, his eyes fixed on the sea chest that Barbara had painted (number sixty-one) cream, fire-engine red inside. The rotating retrogressions beneath his ribs were not alarming at all, nor were the whisper of violas. Was the bakery open? Afternoon shadows (the color of iron ore) darkened the window. Where was the alarm clock? Was it hers? Or his? He opened the utility drawer stuffed with balls of string and extension cords wrapped in stiffened rubber bands. Under stray recipes he found the noisy little red clock – it was five past five. The itinerant baker might be, might not be. Maybe the kebob and chip place was? Hungering for…? What? He considered boiled eggs or fried eggs, aloof eggs with toasted soldiers. Ira loosened other garments, freed himself up. He discarded the red leather jacket. The red day was ending, ribaldry complete. Electrical impulses were beginning to quiet down across neuron gaps. He felt keenly, pulled off the stuck boots and was riven by his own odor. He peeled away the turtleneck, compacted it and squeezed it into the boots. He noticed a nicely folded fresh polo shirt on the kitchen table that was mushroom-gray. Still in cellophane underneath the shirt, new dark green (Versace) underwear and new brown socks made of cotton, all of which he unwrapped.

His arrival was so quickly a shambles. A shower? A bath? A nap? A wank? What next? Dead bees were scattered on the windowsill, the queen embalmed in a dusty honeycomb, suspended in shiny amber. Barbara's seismic chart was attached to the window frame with two pushpins. He dipped his pin-

ky into the belly of pork she had left marinating on
the counter, tasted chili pepper, mace and allspice.
He dipped and tasted again. Hunger returned with
a heart-pinching tweak, also, pockets of gas. When
released these pockets popped out like fresh warm
barnyard eggs hatched by a hen. A plenum of fla-
vors filled his mouth. Prancing rights and wrongs
with stinging tails needled his hard head. He licked
at a discovered liver spot on the back of his hand. As
a non-careerist, he had falling and floating thoughts.
Unpacking and re-wrapping Vera's yellow diamond
in cling film, he transferred Vera's macerating purple
plums into a bowl. In the low light he adjusted cush-
ions and stretched out on the couch. His coronary
arteries were padded with gray sticky sludge glistening like silver day glow. On the coffee table, the clay
statuette of Moses, a paperweight. He viewed it as
a low voltage, sleep-enhancing pied piper of piety
leaking relic radiation from the dawn of the universe.
On Ira's cool skin, rhythms radiated toward loose
muscles as minute swords pierced through nerve
shields with cackling frequency like tangled snakes.
More than enough golden orange tinted his cheeks
because of low oxygen circulation. A dark canopy
was met by sweet infantile breathing – vague tuba,
dim trombone. Wanting more, Ira's hands quivered.
When the muscles at the back of his neck relaxed, his
teeth vibrated. He had a hundred thousand dusky
genes, a hundred trillion cells, twenty-three pairs
of chromosomes in every cell. The DNA in each of

his chromosomes had (like Moses) copied itself each time the cell divided. His tissue had (without help) also divided and renewed itself. Had any part of the chromosome been lost by division? Senescent cells were tired, had stopped dividing. Inadmissible (like Mr. Potato Head) lime-green sentries (as yet unborn) challenged the gravitational grip that kept Ira from floating cheekbones first. He was supine, so blended with the couch that not even Barbara from Brooklyn would be able to connect the dots.

END

ACKNOWLEDGEMENTS

A small glass of spiced apple whiskey or a spoonful of Pepto Bismal might assuage after ingesting this book. I gratefully acknowledge: *After Leaving Mr. Mackenzie* by Jean Rhys, Harper & Row, 1931; "Whispering Grass" by Fred Fisher and Doris Fisher, 1940; and offer a perfumed bouquet for generosity and expertise to the following: editor Helle Valborg Goldman; consultant Johanne Rosenthal; publisher TMI Press; author photo Dixie Sheridan. Additionally, as this work has been under construction for a very long time, some wise eyes have glimpsed and given it thought in its various incarnations during these many years. Grateful thanks to G.B., D.D., K.d.F., A.L., B.L., I.V.M.-W., L.M., M.M., A.O., J.R., S.H.S., A.V.; to anyone inadvertently overlooked and to anyone needing a second dose of apple whickey or Pepto Bismal, my appologies.

AUTHOR'S BIO

Internationally known best-selling author Alison Leslie Gold has published fiction including *Clairvoyant, The Imagined Life of Lucia Joyce*. Jay Parini said about it: "A vividly written book that plays daringly in the no-mans-land between biography and fiction." A reviewer in the *New York Times* summed up another novel *The Devil's Mistress: The Diary of Eva Braun, The Woman Who Lived and Died With Hitler* as follows: "It's hard to forget a novel that spreads across the imagination like a mysterious and evil stain." This book was nominated for the National Book Award and has been translated into Greek, Romanian and Hungarian. Her nonfiction writing on the Holocaust and World War II has received special recognition. Among those who have singled her out as a protector and chronicler of Holocaust experiences is Elie Wiesel, who said of her: "Let us give recognition to Alison Gold. Without her and her talent of persuasion, without her writer's talent, too, this poignant account, vibrating with humanity, would not have been written." Her works include *Anne Frank Remembered, The Story of the Woman Who Helped to Hide Anne Frank*, written with and about Miep Gies, who hid Anne Frank and rescued Anne's diary and *Memories of Anne Frank: Reflections of a Childhood Friend*, written for young people about Hannah "Lies" (pronounced "lease") Goslar, Anne Frank's best friend. Both books are international best sellers translated into more than twenty languages. Neither Miep nor Hannah had been willing to tell their entire stories until meeting Alison. Also for young people, *A Special Fate*, about Chiune Sugihara the little-known Japanese diplomat who saved 6,000 Jews and others during the war.

The nonfiction book *Fiet's Vase and Other Stories of Survival, Europe 1939-1945*, 25 interviews with survivors, is her farewell to that subject matter, and, *Love in the Second Act*, 25 true stories of those who have found love later in life, is the first book exploring less dispiriting themes. Most recently she was invited to write a short work for the Cahier Series (Am. Univ. Paris/Sylph Editions) titled *Lost and Found* soon followed by the publication of a literary novel *The Woman Who Brought Matisse Back from the Dead*, as well as a family story of alcoholic intervention for ages 10-13 co-authored with Darin Elliott—*Elephant in the Living Room*, and *The Potato Eater*, a novella telling the story of gay, ex-con Padric McGarry. Her nonfiction work has received awards ranging from the Best of the Best Award given by the American Library Association, to a Merit of Educational Distinction Award by the Anti-Defamation League, and a Christopher Award affirming the highest values of the human spirit, among others. She divides her time between New York and an island in Greece. Five of her indelible works have been reissued with new material by innovative TMI Publishing, Providence, RI.

www.ingramcontent.com/pod-product-compliance
Lightning Source LLC
Chambersburg PA
CBHW031533040426
42445CB00010B/520